Web Style Guide
Second edition

Web Style Guide

Basic Design Principles for Creating Web Sites
Second edition

Patrick J. Lynch
Yale University Center for Advanced Instructional Media

Sarah Horton
Dartmouth College

Yale University Press
New Haven and London

Printed in Italy by Grafiche SiZ.

Library of Congress Cataloging-in-Publication Data

Lynch, Patrick J. 1953–
Web style guide: basic design principles for creating web sites /
Patrick J. Lynch, Sarah Horton.—2nd ed.
p.   cm.
Includes bibliographic references (p.   ) and index.
ISBN 0-300-09682-8 (cloth : alk. paper)
ISBN 0-300-08898-1 (paper : alk. paper)
1. Web sites—Design. I. Horton, Sarah, 1962– . II. Title.
TK5105.888 .L96 2002
005.7′2—dc21   2001005244

A catalogue record for this book is available from the British Library.

The paper in this book meets the guidelines for permanence and durability
of the Committee on Production Guidelines for Book Longevity
of the Council on Library Resources.

10 9 8 7 6 5 4 3 2 1

For Cheryl and Devorah
—PL

For my son (sun), Nico
—SH

Contents

Foreword

HAVE YOU HEARD of the World Wide Web? If so, your understanding of this exciting new medium has probably evolved somewhat over the past few years. Here is a common evolutionary trajectory:

1 What is this Web thing?
2 The Web is just a flash in the pan.
3 The Web is actually pretty cool.
4 Hmmm, maybe we can make money on the Web.
5 The Web is the cornerstone of the New Economy.
6 There is no New Economy.
7 What was that Web thing?

When things change this fast, humans have a hard time adapting, keeping up, and just plain understanding what's going on. But people's reactions to the Web changed so fast *precisely* because so few of us really understood what it is. In fact, most of us didn't have the time to think hard about how Web sites could truly be useful and good things and how important sound design principles are to making them so.

Frenzied anxiety forced us to rush to legions of "experts" who played upon our fears that "we didn't get it." Through hype and jargon (not to mention wildly creative business modeling), they bullied us back to where we are today: square one.

As we return to the drawing board to figure out what we should do with the Web and our Web sites, what we needed all along becomes clear: fundamentals and fundamentally sound advice to help us think for ourselves and design for our users.

Fortunately, this wonderful little book is still here to show us those fundamentals. Patrick Lynch and Sarah Horton aren't trying to scare you with hype or jargon. They're just trying to get you to slow down, take a deep breath, and think for yourself. They'll teach you basic design principles as well as tricks of the trade, ranging from interaction design to typography, so that you can develop your own Web site or better understand and communicate with the people who are doing that work for you. More important, they will give you a broad framework that will help you understand the Big Picture of Web design. Even if you don't agree with all of their advice, you'll have a starting point from which to develop your ideas and practices.

If you're new to the Web, this is the book for you. It will give you a broad overview of a very complicated subject and get you started in the right direction. It will also make you look very smart when you carry it into meetings with your Web team.

And if you're battle-scarred, weary, and preparing mentally to do battle again, this is the book for you. It will help you synthesize what you've learned over these past few years and reshape your approach to Web site design from a more reasoned and realistic perspective. And it will also make you look very smart when you carry it into meetings with your Web team.

Now get back to it!

-Louis Rosenfeld

Preface to the Second Edition

AS IS THE CASE WITH MANY innovations, the Web has gone through a period of extremes. At its inception, the Web was all about information. Visual design was accidental at best. Web pages were clumsily assembled, and "sites" were accumulations of hyperlinked documents lacking structure or coherence. Designers then took over and crafted attractive, idiosyncratic, and often baffling containers for information. The Web became a better-looking place, but many users hit up against barriers of large graphics, complex layouts, and nonstandard coding. Every site was different, and each required users to relearn how to use the Web, because "real" designers could not be bound by standards or conventions. Instead, designers pushed the boundaries of HTML, using workarounds, kludges, and sleight of hand to design on the cutting edge.

Today, the field of Web design is seen much more as a craft than an art, where function takes precedence over form and content is king. Innovative designs using fancy navigational doodads are generally seen as an annoyance standing between the user and what he or she seeks. Large graphic eye-candy, no matter how pleasing, is simply wasted bandwidth. Like 1960s architecture, much of yesterday's Web design now makes users wince and wonder how it could ever have been fashionable. Instead, today's Web designers are also information architects and usability engineers, and a user-centered design approach is the key to a successful Web site. Instead of constantly requiring users to relearn the Web, sites are beginning to look more alike and to employ the same metaphors and conventions. The Web has now become an everyday thing whose design should not make users think.

The guidance we offer in *Web Style Guide* has always been grounded on the functional aspects of design. In this second edition we extend our focus on functionality with additional sections on Web site accessibility, Cascading Style Sheets, and flexible page design. We include additional sections on information architecture, site maintenance, and multimedia design. And we have added illustrations and updated our Web site examples to reflect current best practices.

In addition to all those who contributed to the first edition of *Web Style Guide*, and whom we acknowledge at the end of the first edition preface (see page xiv), we thank Jean Thomson Black, Laura Jones Dooley, Joyce Ippolito, Maureen Noonan, Nancy Ovedovitz, Deborah Patton, and Amy Steffen at Yale University Press for their hard and high-quality efforts in producing this second edition. We are particularly grateful to Lou Rosenfeld for supplying such a lively and cogent foreword.

I extend heartfelt thanks to my friends and colleagues at Yale Center for Advanced Instructional Media and the School of Medicine's Web Design and

Development unit: Carl Jaffe, Phillip Simon, Sean Jackson, Kimberly Pasko, Jim Soha, Janet Miller, Victor Velt, Crystal Gooding, Michael Flynt, Kathryn Latimer, Venkat Reddy, and Russell Shaddox. In particular, I'd like to thank Carl Jaffe for fifteen years of friendship, wise counsel, and practical advice, much of which now appears on these pages. I'd also like to acknowledge and thank my co-author and dear friend Sarah Horton for her friendship, for her partnership in this enterprise, and for convincing me that converting our *Web Style Guide* site into a book was a good idea.

I am especially grateful to the following individuals for their comments, suggestions, assistance, and counsel over the development of this book and companion Web site: Anne Altemus, Emmett Barkley, Richard Beebe, David Bolinsky, Stephen Cohen, Frank Gallo, Scott Hines, Peter Kindlmann, Howard Newstadt, John Paton, Noble Proctor, Stacy Ruwe, Virginia Simon, William Stewart, Lynna Stone-Infeld, Jan Taylor, Frans Wackers, and Cheryl Warfield.

~PL

I thank my excellent colleagues in Curricular Computing at Dartmouth College: Jeffrey Bohrer, Malcolm Brown, Barbara Knauff, Mark O'Neil, Susan Simon. I also thank the Dartmouth faculty whose sites we use as examples: Joan Campbell, Sheila Culbert, Eva Fodor, Karen Gocsik, Sally Hair, Julie Kalish, Allen Koop, Thomas Luxon, and Gerard Russo. Finally, I am grateful to Andrew Kirkpatrick at the CPB/WGBH National Center for Accessible Media (ncam.wgbh.org) for casting a knowledgable eye on the sections on Web site accessibility.

~SH

Preface to the First Edition

THIS BOOK IS FOR ALL THOSE who wish to publish durable content on the Web. Durable content is not guided by trends; good design will withstand the test of time, whereas trends quickly become frivolous. Success in Web design goes beyond technology and fashion. To create Web sites that endure you need only to communicate your ideas clearly and effectively to your readers.

Though still young, the World Wide Web has already undergone several transformations. The framers of the Web were scientists who wanted to create a device-independent method for exchanging documents. They devised HTML (HyperText Markup Language) as a method for "marking up" the structure of documents to allow for exchange and comparison. Their focus was on the structural logic of documents, not the visual logic of graphic design.

But the Web quickly caught on as a publishing medium; no communication device is more inexpensive or far-reaching. As a tool for communication, however, Web authoring with HTML has limitations. With their focus on the structure of documents, the originators of the Web ignored those visual aspects of information delivery that are critical to effective communication. Once the Web was established as a viable publishing medium, these limitations became obvious and cumbersome. Pages that conformed to HTML standards lacked visual appeal, showing little evidence of the past five centuries of progress in print design. Graphic designers took this relatively primitive authoring and layout tool and began to bend and adapt it to a purpose it was never intended to serve: graphic page design.

The Web viewing audience was also beginning to refine its tastes. The pioneering Web "surfers" who were content to skim the surface of Internet documents are now outnumbered. People are turning to the Web for information—information with depth, breadth, and integrity.

Our purpose for writing this book is to offer basic design principles that you can use to make your content as easy to understand as possible. We explain how to use design as a tool, not as an objective; your Web design should be almost transparent to the reader. We show you how to create a user interface that will allow visitors to your site to navigate your content with ease. We offer suggestions on how to write Web documents; this is a new genre with its own style and guidelines. We delve deep into Web images—color, resolution, compression, and formats—and discuss the benefits of publishing images on the Web. We cover the stylistic and technical issues surrounding the addition of dynamic media to your Web site. All the guidance we offer shares a single purpose: to make your message clear to your readers.

This is not an HTML manual, nor is it a book on graphic design. It is a practical guide to help you design Web sites for the long run.

Many people have given generously of their time and advice during the preparation of this book and of the Web site that preceded the book. At Yale University Press we extend our warmest thanks to Jean Thomson Black, Laura Jones Dooley, and James J. Johnson. We also thank Craig Locatis, Donald Norman, and Edward Tufte for their valuable contributions.

I extend heartfelt thanks to my friends and colleagues at Yale University Center for Advanced Instructional Media: Carl Jaffe, Phillip Simon, Sean Jackson, Kimberly Pasko, Marsha Vazquez, and Jeff Colket. In particular, I'd like to thank Carl Jaffe for over ten years of friendship, wise counsel, and practical advice, much of which now appears on these pages. I'd also like to acknowledge and thank my co-author and good friend Sarah Horton for her friendship, for her partnership in this enterprise, and for convincing me that converting our *Web Style Guide* site into a book was a good idea.

I am especially grateful to the following individuals for their comments, suggestions, assistance, and counsel over the development of this book and companion Web site: Anne Altemus, Emmett Barkley, Richard Beebe, David Bolinsky, Stephen Cohen, Frank Gallo, Kathryn Latimer, Howard Newstadt, Noble Proctor, Lynna Stone-Infeld, Jan Taylor, Mi Young Toh, Tom Urtz, and Cheryl Warfield.

-PL

I thank my co-author, Patrick Lynch, for asking me to join him as co-author of the second edition of the online *Web Style Guide*. Little did he know where that invitation would lead, and I am grateful for his unfailing friendship and good humor throughout the development of this book. I am deeply indebted to Pat and his colleagues at Yale University Center for Advanced Instructional Media for taking me in some years back and teaching me how to see.

I am indebted to my many colleagues and friends at Dartmouth College for their support, suggestions, and counsel, especially John Hawkins, Sheila Culbert, D. Randall Spydell, Ned Holbrook, and Robert M. Murray. I also thank the faculty whose sites appear in this book: Joan Campbell, Eva Fodor, Sally Hair, Allen Koop, Thomas Luxon, and Gerard Russo.

I also thank Malcolm Brown for his steadfast support.

-SH

1   *Process*

In the long run men hit only what they aim at.
—Henry David Thoreau

THE FIRST STEP in designing any Web site is to define your goals. Without a clearly stated mission and objectives the project will drift, bog down, or continue past an appropriate endpoint. Careful planning and a clear purpose are the keys to success in building Web sites, particularly when you are working as part of a development team.

BEFORE YOU BEGIN

Planning a Web site is a two-part process: first you gather your development partners, analyze your needs and goals, and work through the development process outlined here to refine your plans. The second part is creating a site specification document that details what you intend to do and why, what technology and content you'll need, how long the process will take, what you will spend to do it, and how you will assess the results of your efforts. The site specification document is crucial to creating a successful site, as it is both the blueprint for your process and the touchstone you'll use to keep the project focused on your agreed goals and deliverables.

PLANNING

Web sites are developed by groups of people to meet the needs of other groups of people. Unfortunately, Web projects are often approached as a "technology problem," and projects are colored from the beginning by enthusiasms for particular Web techniques or browser plug-ins (Flash, digital media, XML, databases, etc.), not by real human or business needs. People are the key to successful Web projects. To create a substantial site you'll need content experts, writers, information architects, graphic designers, technical experts, and a producer or committee chair responsible for seeing the project to completion. If your site is successful it will have to be genuinely useful to your target audience, meeting their needs and expectations without being too hard to use.

Although the people who will actually use your site will determine whether the project is a success, ironically, those very users are the people least likely to be present and involved when your site is designed and built. Remember that the site development team should always function as an active, committed advocate for the users and their needs. Experienced committee warriors may be skeptical here: these are fine sentiments, but can you really do this in the face of management pressures, budget limitations, and divergent stakeholder interests? Yes, you can—because you have no choice if you really want your Web project to succeed. If you listen only to management directives, keep the process sealed tightly within your development team, and dictate to imagined users what the team imagines is best for them, be prepared for failure. Involve real users, listen and respond to what they say, test your designs with them, and keep the site easy to use, and the project will be a success.

What are your goals? A short statement identifying two or three goals should be the foundation of your Web site design. The statement should include specific strategies around which the Web site will be designed, how long the site design, construction, and evaluation periods will be, and specific quantitative and qualitative measures of how the success of the site will be evaluated. Building a Web site is an ongoing process, not a one-time project with static content. Long-term editorial management and technical maintenance must be covered in your budget and production plans for the site. Without this perspective your electronic publication will suffer the same fate as many corporate communications initiatives—an enthusiastic start without lasting accomplishments.

Know your audience The next step is to identify the potential readers of your Web site so that you can structure the site design to meet their needs and expectations. The knowledge, background, interests, and needs of users will vary from tentative novices who need a carefully structured introduction to expert "power users" who may chafe at anything that seems to patronize them or delay their access to information. A well-designed system should be able to accommodate a range of users' skills and interests. For example, if the goal of your Web site is to deliver internal corporate information, human resources documents, or other information formerly published in paper manuals, your audience will range from those who will visit the site many times every day to those who refer only occasionally to the site.

Design critiques Each member of a site development team will bring different goals, preferences, and skills to the project. Once the team has reached agreement on the mission and goals of the project, consensus on the overall design approach for the Web site needs to be established. The goal at this stage is to identify potential successful models in other Web sites and to begin to *see the design problem from the site user's point of view.*

Unfortunately, production teams rarely include members of the target audience for the Web site. And it is often difficult for team members who are not already experienced site designers to articulate their specific preferences, except in reference to existing sites. Group critiques are a great way to explore what makes a Web site successful, because everyone on the team sees each site from a user's point of view. Have each team member bring a list of a few favorite sites to the critique, and ask them to introduce their sites and comment on the successful elements of each design. In this way you will learn one another's design sensibilities and begin to build consensus on the experience that your audience will have when they visit the finished site.

Content inventory   Once you have an idea of your Web site's mission and general structure, you can begin to assess the content you will need to realize your plans. Building an inventory or database of existing and needed content will force you to take a hard look at your existing content resources and to make a detailed outline of your needs. Once you know where you are short on content you can concentrate on those deficits and avoid wasting time on areas with existing resources that are ready to use. A clear grasp of your needs will also help you develop a realistic schedule and budget for the project. Content development is the hardest, most time-consuming part of any Web site development project. Starting early with a firm plan in hand will help ensure that you won't be caught later with a well-structured but empty Web site.

DEVELOPING A SITE SPECIFICATION

The site specification is the planning team's concise statement of core goals, values, and intent, to provide the ultimate policy direction for everything that comes next. Designing a substantial Web site is a costly and time-consuming process. When you're up to your neck in the daily challenges of building the site, it can be surprisingly easy to forget why you are doing what you are, to lose sight of your original priorities, and to not know on any given day whether the detailed decisions you are making actually support those overall goals and objectives. A well-written site specification is a powerful daily tool for judging the effectiveness of a development effort. It provides the team with a compass to keep the development process focused on the ultimate purposes of the site. As such, it quickly becomes a daily reference point to settle disputes, to judge the potential utility of new ideas as they arise, to measure progress, and to keep the development team focused on the ultimate goals.

At minimum, a good site specification should define the content scope, budget, schedule, and technical aspects of the Web site. The best site specifications are very short and to the point, and are often just outlines or bullet lists of the major design or technical features planned. The finished site specification should contain the goals statement from the planning phase, as well as the structural details of the site:

Goals and strategies
- What is the mission of your organization?
- How will creating a Web site support your mission?
- What are your two or three most important goals for the site?

- Who is the primary audience for the Web site?
- What do you want the audience to think or do after having visited your site?
- What Web-related strategies will you use to achieve those goals?
- How will you measure the success of your site?
- How will you adequately maintain the finished site?

Production issues
- How many pages will the site contain? What is the maximum acceptable count under this budget?
- What special technical or functional requirements are needed?
- What is the budget for the site?
- What is the production schedule for the site, including intermediate milestones and dates?
- Who are the people or vendors on the development team and what are their responsibilities?

These are big questions, and the broad conceptual issues are too often dismissed as committees push toward starting the "real work" of designing and building a Web site. However, if you cannot confidently answer all of these questions, then no amount of design or production effort can guarantee a useful result.

Avoiding "scope creep"   The site specification defines the scope of your project—that is, what and how much you need to do, the budget, and the development schedule. "Scope creep" is the most prevalent cause of Web project failures. In badly planned projects, scope creep is the gradual but inexorable process by which previously unplanned "features" are added, content and features are padded to mollify each stakeholder group, major changes in content or site structure during site construction are made, and more content or interactive functionality than you originally agreed to create is stuffed in. No single overcommitment is fatal, but the slow, steady accumulation of additions and changes is often enough to blow budgets, ruin schedules, and bury what might have been an elegant original plan under megabytes of muddle and confusion.

Don't leap into building a Web site before you understand what you want to accomplish and before you have developed a solid and realistic site specification for creating your Web site. The more carefully you plan, the better off you will be when you begin to build your site.

One excellent way to keep a tight rein on the overall scope of the site content is to specify a maximum page count in the site specification. Although a page count is hardly infallible as a guide (after all, Web pages can be arbitrarily long), it serves as a constant reminder to everyone involved of the project's intended scope. If the page count goes up, make it a rule to revisit the budget implications automatically—the cold realities of budgets and schedules will often cool the enthusiasm to stuff in "just one more page." A good way to keep a lid on scope creep is to treat the page count as a "zero sum game." If someone wants to add pages, it's up to them to nominate other pages to remove or to obtain a corresponding increase in the budget and schedule to account for the increased work involved.

Changes and refinements can be a good thing, as long as everyone is realistic about the impact of potential changes on the budget and schedule of a project. Any substantial change to the planned content, design, or technical aspects of a site must be tightly coupled with a revision of the budget and schedule of the project. People are often reluctant to discuss budgets or deadlines frankly and will often agree to substantial changes or additions to a development plan rather than face an awkward conversation with a client or fellow team member. But this acquiescence merely postpones the inevitable damage of not dealing with scope changes rationally.

The firm integration of schedule, budget, and scope is the only way to keep a Web project from becoming unhinged from the real constraints of time, money, and the ultimate quality of the result. A little bravery and honesty up front can save you much grief later. Make the plan carefully, and then stick to it.

THE SITE DEVELOPMENT PROCESS

Every significant Web project poses unique challenges, but the overall process of developing a complex Web site generally follows six major stages:

1 Site definition and planning
2 Information architecture
3 Site design
4 Site construction
5 Site marketing
6 Tracking, evaluation, and maintenance

Developing a large Web site is a process that may have far-reaching budgetary, personnel, and public relations consequences for an organization, both during the development of the site and long after its successful deployment. Too many Web sites begin life as ad hoc efforts, created by small interest groups working in isolation from their peers elsewhere in the organization and without fully considering the site's goals within the context of the organization's overall mission. The result of poorly planned, hasty development efforts often is an "orphan site," starved of resources and attention.

As you consider the development process outlined below, note that the construction of the pages that make up the Web site is one of the last things that takes place in a well-designed project. Consider each step in the process, and its impact on your developing site specification plan. Think before you act, and make sure you have the organizational backing, budget, and personnel resources you'll need to make the project a success.

1   SITE DEFINITION AND PLANNING
This initial stage is where you define your goals and objectives for the Web site and begin to collect and analyze the information you'll need to justify the budget and resources required. This is also the time to define the scope of the site content, the interactive functionality and technology support required, and the depth and breadth of information resources that you will need to fill out the site and meet your reader's expectations. If you are contracting out the production of the Web site, you will also need to interview and select a site design firm. Ideally, your site designers should be involved as soon as possible in the planning discussions.

Site production checklist   Not every site will require consideration of every item below. Developers within corporations or other large enterprises can often count on substantial in-house technology support when creating new Web sites. If you are on your own as an individual or small business, you may need to contract with various technology and design vendors to assemble everything you'll need to create a substantial content site or small e-commerce site.

Production
- Will your site production team be composed of in-house people, outside contractors, or a mix of the two?
- Who will manage the process?
- Who are your primary content experts?
- Who will be the liaison to any outside contractors?
- Who will function long-term as the Webmaster or senior site editor?

Technology
- What browsers and operating systems should your site support?
    Windows, Macintosh, UNIX, Linux
    Netscape Navigator, Internet Explorer; minimum version supported
- Network bandwidth of average site visitors
    Internal audience or largely external audience?
    Ethernet or high-speed connections typical of corporate offices
    ISDN, or DSL medium-speed connections typical of suburban homes
    Modem connections for rural, international, or poorer audiences
- Dynamic HTML (HyperText Markup Language) and advanced features?
    JavaScript or VBSCRIPT required
    Java applets required
    Style sheets required
    Third-party browser plug-ins required

Special features of the UNIX or NT server environments required
Special security or confidentiality features required
- How will readers reach the support personnel?
Email messages from readers
Chat rooms, forums, help desks, or phone support
- Database support?
User log-ins required to enter any site areas?
Questionnaires required?
Search and retrieval from databases needed?
- Audiovisual content
Video or audio productions?

Web server support
- In-house Web server or outsourced to Internet Service Provider (ISP)?
Unique domain names available (multihoming)
Disk space or site traffic limitations or extra costs
Adequate capacity to meet site traffic demands?
Twenty-four-hour, seven-days-a-week support and maintenance?
Statistics on users and site traffic?
Server log analysis: in-house or outsourced?
Search engine suitable for your content?
CGI (Common Gateway Interface), programming, and database middle-ware support available?
Database support or coordination with in-house staff?

Budgeting
- Salaries and benefits for short-term development staff and long-term editorial and support staff
- Hardware and software for in-house development team members
- Staff training in Web use, database, Web marketing, and Web design
- Outsourcing fees
Site design and development
Technical consulting
Database development
Site marketing
- Ongoing personnel support for site
Site editor or Webmaster
- Ongoing server and technical support
- Database maintenance and support
- New content development and updating

Appoint a site editor   A site that is "everyone's responsibility" can quickly become an orphan. A maintenance plan should specify who is responsible for the content of each page in the site. To maintain consistent editorial, graphic design, and management policies you'll also need one person to act as the editor of the overall Web site. The site editor's duties will vary according to how you choose to maintain your site. Some editors do all the work of maintaining site content, relieving their coworkers of the need to deal directly with Web page editing. Other editors coordinate and edit the work of many contributors who work directly on the site pages. If multiple people contribute to site maintenance, the site editor may choose to edit pages after they are created and posted to avoid becoming a bottleneck in the communications process. However, high-profile public pages or pages that contain very important content should be vetted by the editor before public posting.

In addition to ensuring editorial quality, a site editor must also ensure that the content of the site reflects the policies of the enterprise, is consistent with local appropriate use policies, and does not contain material that violates copyright laws. Many people who post pictures, cartoons, music files, or written material copied from other sites on their own sites do not understand copyrights and the legal risks in using copyrighted materials inappropriately. A site editor is often an institution's first line of defense against an expensive lawsuit over the misuse of protected material.

2 INFORMATION ARCHITECTURE

At this stage you need to detail the content and organization of the Web site. The team should inventory all existing content, describe what new content is required, and define the organizational structure of the site. Once a content architecture has been sketched out, you should build small prototypes of parts of the site to test what it feels like to move around within the design. Site prototypes are useful for two reasons. First, they are the best way to test site navigation and develop the user interface. The prototypes should incorporate enough pages to assess accurately what it's like to move from menus to content pages. Second, creating a prototype allows the graphic designers to develop relations between how the site looks and how the navigation interface supports the information design. The key to good prototyping is flexibility early on: the site prototypes should not be so complex or elaborate that the team becomes too invested in one design at the expense of exploring better alternatives.

Typical results or contract deliverables at the end of this stage could include:

- Detailed site design specification
- Detailed description of site content
    Site maps, thumbnails, outlines, table of contents
- Detailed technical support specification
    Browser technology supported
    Connection speed supported
    Web server and server resources

- Proposals to create programming or technology to support specific features of the site
- A schedule for implementing the site design and construction
- One or more site prototypes of multiple pages
- Multiple graphic design and interface design sketches or roughs

3 SITE DESIGN

At this stage the project acquires its look and feel, as the page grid, page design, and overall graphic design standards are created and approved. Now the illustrations, photography, and other graphic or audiovisual content for the site need to be commissioned and created. Research, writing, organizing, assembling, and editing the site's text content is also performed at this stage. Any programming, database design and data entry, and search engine design should be well under way by now. The goal is to produce all the content components and functional programming and have them ready for the final production stage: the construction of the actual Web site pages.

Typical products or contract deliverables at the end of this stage could include:

Content components, detailed organization and assembly
- Text, edited and proofread
- Graphic design specifications for all page types
    Finished interface graphics for page templates
    Header and footer graphics, logos, buttons, backgrounds
- Detailed page comps or finished examples of key pages
    Site graphic standards manual for large, complex sites
- Interface design and master page grid templates completed
    Finished HTML template pages
- Illustrations
- Photography

Functional and logic components
- JavaScript scripts, Java applets designed
- Database tables and programming, interaction prototypes completed
- Search engine designed and tested

Templates   Whether you develop your site on you own or hire a professional Web developer, you should develop page templates for your new Web site. It's much easier to add new pages if you can start from a page that already has the basic navigation and site graphics in place. If you share page development with other people, you will also want to be able to give your team members templates to use, along with instructions on how to handle page text and content graphics according to your standards. Popular Web site development software packages such as Macromedia's Dreamweaver offer powerful templates and standard reusable libraries of site graphics and HTML that make it easy to create new pages and maintain your site.

Accessibility For many organizations, providing equal access to Web pages is institutional policy, if not a federal mandate. It is critical, therefore, that you validate your designs and page templates and the content of your site throughout the development process to ensure that your pages are accessible to all users. To check the accessibility of your pages you can use a tool like Bobby (www.cast.org/bobby). Bobby is a free service provided by the Center for Applied Special Technology. After you supply the URL (Uniform Resource Locator) of your page, Bobby checks the page against the Web Accessibility Initiative guidelines and flags potential barriers for users with disabilities. Bobby also recommends changes that will improve the accessibility of your pages. Check your designs at every development milestone to avoid time-consuming and potentially costly revamping efforts.

4 SITE CONSTRUCTION

Only at this mature stage of the project are the bulk of the site's Web pages constructed and filled out with content. By waiting until you have a detailed site architecture, mature content components, and a polished page design specification you will minimize the content churning, redundant development efforts, and wasted energy that inevitably result from rushing to create pages too soon. Of course, you will always learn new things about your overall design as the prototype matures into the full-blown Web site. Be prepared to refine your designs as you navigate through the growing Web site and discover both weak spots and opportunities to improve navigation or content.

Once the site has been constructed, with all pages completed and all database and programming components linked, it is ready for beta testing. Testing should be done primarily by readers outside your site development team who are willing to supply informed criticism and report programming bugs, typographic errors, and critique the overall design and effectiveness of the site. Fresh users will inevitably notice things that you and your development team have overlooked. Only after the site has been thoroughly tested should you begin to publicize the URL address of the site to a larger audience.

Typical products or contract deliverables at the end of this stage should include:

- Finished HTML for all Web pages, all page content in place
- Finished navigation link structure
- All programming in place and linked to pages, ready for beta testing
- All database components in place and linked to site pages
- All graphic design, illustration, and photography in place
- Final proofreading of all site content

- Detailed testing of database and programming functionality
- Testing and verification of database reporting features
- Testing of site reader support procedures, answering email, etc.
- Archives of all site content components, HTML code, programming code, and any other site development materials

Maintainable code   Most business or departments in larger enterprises will contract with a Web development group to create the initial site design and to build all the pages in the first version of the Web site. They then assume responsibility for the site, doing some or all of the day-to-day maintenance and updating content as needed to keep the site current.

Often not until the practicalities of site maintenance come up do customers realize the importance of understanding the details of how the Web developer generated the HTML and other code that makes up the Web site. Although all HTML is much the same to Web browsing software, how the HTML is formatted and what Web authoring tool the developer used can make a huge difference in how the code looks to a human reader. Consider the two code examples below:

Example 1

```
<!— START OF SCHEDULE TABLE ======= —>
<table summary="Human Investigations Committee II schedule, FY 2001."
border="0" width="100%" cellspacing="0" cellpadding="1">
<tr valign="top">
<!— ============================== —>
<td width="50%">
   <p class="tabletext">
   Deadline for Submissions</p>
</td>
<td width="2%" >
    
</td>
<td width="48%" >
   <p class="tabletext">
 Meeting Dates 2001</p>
</td></tr>
<!— ============================== —>
```

Example 2

```
<table summary="Human Investigations Committee II schedule, FY 2001."
border="0" width="100%" cellspacing="0" cellpadding="1"><tr
valign="top"><td width="50%"><p class="tabletext">Deadline for
Submissions</p></td><td width="2%"> </td><td width="48%" > <p
class="tabletext">Meeting Dates 2001</p></td></tr>
```

Which example do you find easier to understand? These code examples are exactly equivalent to Web browser software, but most *people* would find Example 1 significantly easier to read and understand. If you contract with a developer to build your site, it is crucial to understand how the developer writes code, what state the code will be in when the site is delivered, and whether the software used by the developer is compatible with what you will be using to maintain the site after delivery. Some Web development software produces HTML code that is nearly impossible for a human to read without significant (and expensive) reformatting. Other programs (such as Macromedia Dreamweaver) produce HTML code that is easy for Web programmers to read, which can make a huge difference if you decide to change Web developers or if you decide to edit HTML directly in maintaining your site. If you hire someone to create your Web site, be sure to ask what tools he or she will use to write the HTML and any other code. Ask to see examples of HTML code written for other clients. Check the code to be sure the developer inserts explanatory comments and dividers for legibility in the code. Be sure you understand whether there will be any problems or conflicts in using your favorite Web tools to edit the HTML code your Web developer produces.

5 SITE MARKETING

Your Web site should be an integral part of all marketing campaigns and corporate communications programs, and the URL for your site should appear on every piece of correspondence and marketing collateral your organization generates.

If your Web site is aimed primarily at local audiences you must look beyond getting listed in standard Web indexes, such as Yahoo and Infoseek, URL and publicize your URL where local residents or businesses will encounter it. Local libraries (and schools, where the content is relevant) are often the key to publicizing a new Web site within a localized geographic area.

You may also find opportunities to cross-promote your site with affiliated businesses, professional organizations, broadcast or print media, visitor or local information agencies, real estate and relocation services, Internet access providers, and local city or town directory sites. Your organization could also feature local nonprofit charitable or school events on your Web site. The cost in server space is usually trivial, and highly publicized local events featuring a Web page hosted within your site will boost local awareness of your Web presence. Site sponsorship might also interest local broadcast media as an interesting story angle.

Your home page URL should appear in all:

- Print advertisements
- Radio and television advertisements
- Lobby kiosks in high-traffic areas of your enterprise or in local libraries, schools, or other suitable venues
- Direct mail campaigns
- Business cards
- Stationery
- Bills and statements

- Product manuals and product packaging
- Response cards and warrantee cards
- Publications and promotional materials
- Press releases
- Posters and billboards

6 TRACKING, EVALUATION, AND MAINTENANCE

An abundance of information about visitors to your site can be recorded with your Web server software. Even the simplest site logs track how many people (unique visitors) saw your site over a given time, how many pages were requested for viewing, and many other variables. By analyzing the server logs for your Web site you can develop quantitative data on the success of your site. The logs will tell you what pages were the most popular and what brands and versions of Web browser people used to view your site. Server logs can also give you information on the geographic location of your site readers. The usefulness of your site logs will depend on what you ask of the server and the people who maintain the server. Detailed logs are the key to quantifying the success of a Web site. Your Webmaster should archive all site logs for long-term analysis and should be prepared to add or change the information categories being logged as your needs and interests change.

A number of popular software packages are designed to produce easily readable site traffic reports, complete with data graphics and charts to aid in data analysis. As a service to customers, site hosting companies often offer reports from popular site analysis programs like WebTrends, often free of charge. Before contracting with an Internet Service Provider (ISP) for site hosting services, always ask about site analysis services. If your ISP or corporate Web site does not offer a good site traffic analysis package, ask whether the Webmaster can give you access to a monthly server log of your account. Basic versions of traffic analysis programs like WebTrends cost about three hundred dollars, and you can run them on a personal computer if you can gain access to the raw Web server log from your ISP or corporate Webmaster.

Maintaining the site   Don't abandon your site once the production "goes live" and the parties are over. The aesthetic and functional aspects of a large Web site need constant attention and grooming, particularly if a group of individuals shares responsibility for updating content. Someone will need to be responsible for coordinating and vetting the new content stream, maintaining the graphic and editorial standards, and assuring that the programming and linkages of all pages remain intact and functional. Links on the Web are perishable, and you'll need to check periodically that links to pages outside your immediate site are still working. Don't let your site go stale by starving it of resources just as you begin to develop an audience—if you disappoint them by not following through it will be doubly difficult to attract them back.

Backups and site archives   The site editor should be sure that the Web site is regularly backed up onto a secure and reliable storage medium to ensure that a catastrophic hardware failure in your Web server does not wipe out your Web site. Most Web servers maintained by information technology professionals or commercial Web service providers are backed up at least once a day. If you don't know what your particular backup schedule is, ask your Webmaster or Web services vendor. Human error is the most common reason you may want quick access to a backup copy of your Web site. Unfortunately, it's easy to accidentally overwrite an old file (or a whole directory of files) over a newer version on the Web server, to delete something important in error, or to inadvertently wipe out someone else's work when updating a Web site. A recent backup (ideally no more than twenty-four hours old) can often be a lifesaver in correcting a mistake.

If your site is successful, it will quickly become an important record of your enterprise's work, your accomplishments, and a valuable record of the "state of things" as the site evolves over time. Unfortunately, too little attention is paid to this aspect of Web sites, and we are collectively losing huge pieces of our history because no one thinks about preserving permanent records of a Web site. Unless your Web site is prohibitively large, your Web site editor could arrange to collect and store the files of the site periodically or contract with your Web service provider to set aside a backup version at regular intervals so that it can be stored for long-term use. We take for granted the "paper trail" of history left by conventional business and work practices. Without a plan for preserving our digital works, our collective history may vanish without a trace.

REFERENCES

DEVELOPMENT PROCESS

Burdman, Jessica R. 1999. *Collaborative Web development: Strategies and best practices for Web teams*. Reading, Mass.: Addison-Wesley.

Dobson, Michael Singer. 1996. *Practical project management: Secrets of managing any project on time and on budget*. Mission, Kans.: SkillPath.

Frenza, J. P., and Michelle Szabo. *Web and new media pricing guide: A business and pricing guide for Web sites and related digital media*. Indianapolis, Ind.: Hayden Books.

Friedlein, Ashley. 2001. *Web project management: Delivering successful commercial Web sites*. San Francisco: Morgan Kaufmann.

Graphic Artists Guild et al. 1997. *Graphic Artists Guild handbook: Pricing and ethical guidelines*, 9th ed. Cincinnati, Ohio: North Light Books.

Reiss, Eric L. 2000. *Practical information architecture: A hands-on approach to structuring successful Web sites*. Reading, Mass.: Addison-Wesley.

Siegel, David. 1997. *Secrets of successful Web sites: Project management on the World Wide Web*. Indianapolis, Ind.: Hayden Books.

Veen, Jeffrey. 2001. *The art and science of Web design*. Indianapolis, Ind.: New Riders.

GENERAL REFERENCE

Meyer, Eric. A. 2000. *Cascading Style Sheets: The definitive guide*. Sebastopol, Calif.: O'Reilly.

Musciano, Chuck, and Bill Kennedy. 2000. HTML *and* XHTML: *The definitive guide*. Sebastopol, Calif.: O'Reilly.

Niederst, Jennifer. 1999. *Web design in a nutshell: A desktop quick reference*. Sebastopol, Calif.: O'Reilly.

Powell, Thomas A. 2000. *Web design: The complete reference*. Berkeley, Calif.: Osborne/McGraw-Hill.

Spainhour, Steven, and Robert Eckstein. 1999. *Webmaster in a nutshell: A desktop quick reference*, 2d ed. Sebastopol, Calif.: O'Reilly.

2   *Interface Design*

The capacity for perception depends on the amount, the kind and
the availability of past experiences. . . . We see familiar things more
clearly than we see objects about which we have no stock of
memories.
—Aldous Huxley

Users of Web documents don't just look at information, they interact
with it in novel ways that have no precedents in paper document design.
The graphic user interface (GUI) of a computer system comprises the interaction metaphors, images, and concepts used to convey function and meaning on the computer screen. It also includes the detailed visual characteristics of every component of the graphic interface and the functional
sequence of interactions over time that produce the characteristic look and
feel of Web pages and hypertext linked relations. Graphic design and visual
"signature" graphics are not used simply to enliven Web pages—graphics
are integral to the user's experience with your site. In interactive documents
graphic design cannot be separated from issues of interface design.

WEB PAGE DESIGN VERSUS CONVENTIONAL DOCUMENT DESIGN
Concepts about structuring information today stem largely from the organization of printed books and periodicals and the library indexing and catalog
systems that developed around printed information. The "interface standards" of books in the English-speaking world are well established and
widely agreed-upon, and detailed instructions for creating books may be
found in such guides as *The Chicago Manual of Style*. Every feature of the
book, from the contents page to the index, has evolved over the centuries,
and readers of early books faced some of the same organizational problems
that users of hypermedia documents confront today. Gutenberg's Bible of
1456 is often cited as the first modern book, yet even after the explosive
growth of publishing that followed Gutenberg's invention of printing with
movable type, more than a century passed before page numbering, indexes,
tables of contents, and even title pages became expected and necessary features of books. Web documents are undergoing a similar evolution and stan-
dardization.

Design precedents in print   Although networked interactive hypermedia
documents pose novel challenges to information designers, most of the
guidance needed to design, create, assemble, edit, and organize multiple
forms of media does not differ radically from current practice in print media.

Most Web documents can be made to conform to *The Chicago Manual of Style* conventions for editorial style and text organization. Much of what an organization needs to know about creating clear, comprehensive, and consistent internal publishing standards is already available in such publishing guides as the *Xerox Publishing Standards: A Manual of Style and Design*. Don't get so lost in the novelty of Web pages that basic standards of editorial and graphic design are tossed aside.

MAKE YOUR WEB PAGES FREESTANDING

World Wide Web pages differ from books and other documents in one crucial respect: hypertext links allow users to access a single Web page with no preamble. For this reason Web pages need to be more independent than pages in a book. For example, the headers and footers of Web pages should be more informative and elaborate than those on printed pages. It would be absurd to repeat the copyright information, author, and date of a book at the bottom of every printed page, but individual Web pages often need to provide such information because a single Web page may be the only part of a site that some users will see. This problem of making documents freestanding is not unique to Web pages. Journals, magazines, and most newspapers repeat the date, volume number, and issue number at the top or bottom of each printed page because they know that readers often rip out articles or photocopy pages and will need that information to be able to trace the source of the material.

Given the difficulties inherent in creating Web sites that are both easy to use and full of complex content, the best design strategy is to apply a few fundamental document design principles consistently in every Web page you create. The basic elements of a document aren't complicated and have almost nothing to do with Internet technology. It's like a high school journalism class: who, what, when, and where.

Who Who is speaking? This question is so basic, and the information is so often taken for granted, that authors frequently overlook the most fundamental piece of information a reader needs to assess the provenance of a Web document. Whether the page originates from an individual author or an institution, always tell the reader who created it. The flood of Web sites propagating incorrect or intentionally misleading material on the Florida vote problems of the 2000 American presidential election offers a vivid example of how "information" of no known origin and of dubious authenticity can quickly cloud legitimate inquiry and discussion.

What All documents need clear titles to capture the reader's attention, but for several reasons peculiar to the Web this basic editorial element is especially crucial. The document title is often the first thing browsers of World Wide Web documents see as the page comes up. In pages with lots of graphics the title may be the only thing the user sees for several seconds as the graphics download onto the page. In addition, the page title will become the text of a browser "bookmark" if the user chooses to add your page to his or her list of URLs ("Universal Resource Locator," the formal term for Web addresses). A misleading or ambiguous title or one that contains technical gibberish will not help users remember why they bookmarked your page.

When   Timeliness is an important element in evaluating the worth of a document. We take information about the age of most paper documents for granted: newspapers, magazines, and virtually all office correspondence is dated. Date every Web page, and change the date whenever the document is updated. This is especially important in long or complex online documents that are updated regularly but may not look different enough to signal a change in content to occasional readers. Corporate information, personnel manuals, product information, and other technical documents delivered as Web pages should always carry version numbers or revision dates. Remember that many readers prefer to print long documents from the Web. If you don't include revision dates your audience may not be able to assess whether the version they have in hand is current.

Where   The Web is an odd "place" that has huge informational dimensions but few explicit cues to the place of origin of a document. Click on a Web link, and you could be connected to a Web server in Sydney, Chicago, or Rome—anywhere, in fact, with an Internet connection. Unless you are well versed in parsing URLs it can be hard to tell where a page originates. This is the *World Wide* Web, after all, and the question of where a document comes from is sometimes inseparable from whom the document comes from. Always tell the reader where you are from, with (if relevant) your corporate or institutional affiliations.

Incorporating the "home" URL on at least the main pages of your site is an easy way to maintain the connection to where a page originated. Once the reader has saved the page as a text file or printed the page onto paper, this connection may be lost. Although newer versions of the most common Web browsers allow users to include the URL automatically in anything they print, many people never take advantage of this optional feature. Too many of us have stacks of printed Web pages with no easy way of locating the Web sites where they originated.

Every Web page needs:
- An informative title (which also becomes the text of any bookmark to the page)
- The creator's identity (author or institution)
- A creation or revision date
- At least one link to a local home page or menu page
- The "home page" URL on the major menu pages in your site

Include these basic elements and you will have traveled 90 percent of the way toward providing your readers with an understandable Web user interface.

BASIC INTERFACE DESIGN

USER-CENTERED DESIGN

Graphic user interfaces were designed to give people control over their personal computers. Users now expect a level of design sophistication from all graphic interfaces, including Web pages. The goal is to provide for the needs of all your potential users, adapting Web technology to their expectations and never requiring readers to conform to an interface that places unnecessary obstacles in their paths.

This is where your research on the needs and demographics of the target audience is crucial. It's impossible to design for an unknown person whose needs you don't understand. Create sample scenarios with different types of users seeking information from your site. Would an experienced user seeking a specific piece of information be helped or hindered by your home page design? Would a casual reader be intimidated by a complex menu scheme? Testing your designs and getting feedback from a variety of users is the best way to see whether your design ideas are giving them what they want from your site.

Clear navigation aids   Most user interactions with Web pages involve navigating hypertext links between documents. The main interface problem in Web sites is the lack of a sense of where you are within the local organization of information:

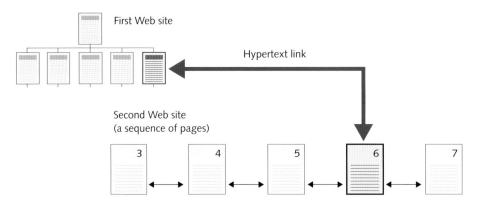

Clear, consistent icons, graphic identity schemes, and graphic or text-based overview and summary screens can give the user confidence that they can find what they are looking for without wasting time.

Users should always be able to return easily to your home page and to other major navigation points in the site. These basic links should be present and in consistent locations on every page. Graphic buttons will provide basic navigation links and create a graphic identity that tells users they are within the site domain. In this site, for example, the graphic header appears on every page:

The button bar is efficient (offering multiple choices in a small space) and predictable (it is always there, at the top of every page), and it provides a consistent graphic identity throughout the site.

No dead-end pages   Web pages often appear with no preamble: readers can make or follow links directly to subsection pages buried deep in the hierarchy of Web sites. They may never see your home page or other introductory site information. If your subsection pages do not contain links to the home page or to local menu pages, the reader will be locked out from the rest of the Web site:

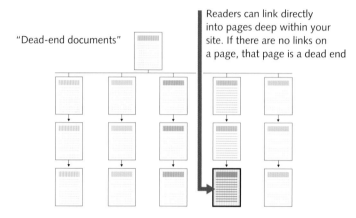

"Dead-end documents"

Readers can link directly into pages deep within your site. If there are no links on a page, that page is a dead end

Make sure all pages in your site have *at minimum* a link back to the main "home" page or, better yet, a home page link along with links to the other sections of the site.

Direct access   Users want to get information in the fewest possible steps. This means that you must design an efficient hierarchy of information to minimize steps through menu pages. Studies have shown that users prefer menus that present at least five to seven links and that they prefer a few very dense screens of choices to many layers of simplified menus. The following table demonstrates that you do not need many levels of menus to incorporate lots of choices:

Number of nested menus	Number of menu items listed			
	5	7	8	10
1	5	7	8	10
2	25	49	64	100
3	125	343	512	1000

Design your site hierarchy so that real content is only a click or two away from the main menu pages of your site.

Bandwidth and interaction Users will not tolerate long delays. Research has shown that for most computing tasks the threshold of frustration is about ten seconds. Web page designs that are not well "tuned" to the network access speed of typical users will only frustrate them. If your users are primarily general public browsers "surfing" the Web via dial-up modem connections, it is foolish to put huge bitmap graphics on your pages—the average modem user will not be patient enough to wait while your graphics download over the phone line. If, however, you are building a university or corporate intranet site where most users will access the Web server at Ethernet speeds or better, you can be much more ambitious in the use of graphics and multimedia. Many home computer users can now use high-speed DSL (digital subscriber line) or cable modems to access the Web. However, industry observers expect that it will be at least another five years before Web designers can count on most home users' having access to high-speed Web connections. In general, be conservative with Web graphics. Even users with high-speed connections appreciate a fast-loading page.

Simplicity and consistency Users are not impressed with complexity that seems gratuitous, especially those users who may be depending on the site for timely and accurate work-related information. Your interface metaphors should be simple, familiar, and logical—if you need a metaphor for information design, choose a genre familiar to readers of documents, such as a book or a library. Highly unusual, "creative" navigation and home page metaphors always fail because they impose an unfamiliar, unpredictable interface burden on the user.

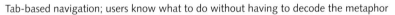

Tab-based navigation; users know what to do without having to decode the metaphor

The user interface for your Web site should follow the general navigation and layout conventions of major Web sites because your users will already be used to those conventions. Users spend most of their time on sites other than yours, so avoid highly unusual interfaces if you wish to attract and keep a large audience.

The best information designs are never noticed. An excellent model of interface design is the Adobe Corporation Web site. Graphic headers act as navigation aids and are consistently applied across every page in the site. Once you know where the standard links are on the page header graphics, the interface becomes almost invisible and navigation is easy:

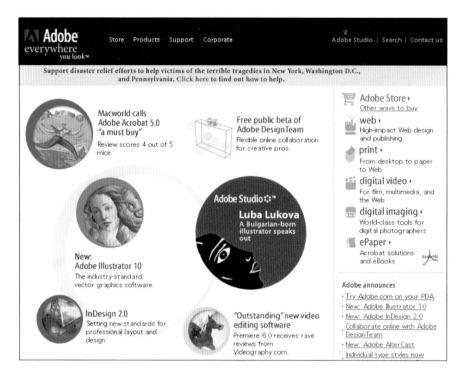

For maximum functionality and legibility, your page and site design should be built on a consistent pattern of modular units that all share the same basic layout grids, graphic themes, editorial conventions, and hierarchies of organization. The goal is to be consistent and predictable; your users should feel comfortable exploring your site and confident that they can find what they need. The graphic identity of a series of pages in a Web site provides visual cues to the continuity of information. The header menu graphics present on every page of the Adobe site create a consistent user interface and corporate identity:

Even if your site design does not employ navigation graphics, a consistent approach to the layout of titles, subtitles, page footers, and navigation links to your home page or related pages will reinforce the reader's sense of context within the site. To preserve the effect of a "seamless" system of pages you may wish to bring important information into your site and adapt it to your page layout scheme rather than using links to send the reader away from your site (be sure there are no copyright restrictions on copying the information into your site).

Design integrity and stability   To convince your users that what you have to offer is accurate and reliable, you will need to design your Web site as carefully as you would any other type of corporate communication, using the same high editorial and design standards. A site that looks sloppily built, with poor visual design and low editorial standards, will not inspire confidence.

Functional stability in any Web design means keeping the interactive elements of the site working reliably. Functional stability has two components: getting things right the first time as you design the site, and then keeping things functioning smoothly over time. Good Web sites are inherently interactive, with lots of links to local pages within the site as well as links to other sites on the Web. As you create your design you will need to check frequently that all of your links work properly. Information changes quickly on the Web, both in your site and in everyone else's. After the site is established you will need to check that your links are still working properly and that the content they supply remains relevant.

Feedback and dialog   Your Web design should offer constant visual and functional confirmation of the user's whereabouts and options, via graphic design, navigation buttons, or uniformly placed hypertext links. Feedback also means being prepared to respond to your users' inquiries and comments. Well-designed Web sites provide direct links to the Web site editor or Webmaster responsible for running the site. Planning for this ongoing relationship with users of your site is vital to the long-term success of the enterprise.

One of the defining principles of the Web is that it should provide all people, regardless of physical or technological readiness, with access to information. Since the Web took off as a visual medium, the goals of design have been at odds with the goals of accessibility. When designers began to use large images, proprietary media formats, and complex page layouts to produce well-designed documents, the Web became a better-looking place, but those users who require clean HTML for access were shut out from many pages. Today, the course of Web design is shifting back to its original purpose. HTML has matured to offer more visual controls, so designers have more tools at hand to create structured and navigable Web sites without resorting to hacks and workarounds. Around the world, initiatives are under way to mandate that disabled users have equal access to Internet resources, including the guidelines issued by the Web Accessibility Initiative (WAI) of the World Wide Web Consortium (W3C) and, in the United States, the amendments to Section 508 of the Rehabilitation Act of 1973. The result is that Web interface design is intricately tied to accessibility design. It is the responsibility of Web designers to understand and support the needs of disabled users.

Alternates and fallbacks   The underlying principle of Web accessibility guidelines is simple: if you provide information in any medium besides plain text, you should always provide an alternate, or *fallback*, version. The notion of fallbacks is at the core of the language of the Web, allowing rich and varied content to transform gracefully under different conditions. It also lies behind the injunction that no content should become outdated and inaccessible because of the progress of technology. To meet these goals, HTML includes methods for providing fallbacks for some types of nontext content.

As an example, one of the beauties of the Web and HTML is the ability to build in "alternate" text descriptions so that users without graphics capabilities can understand the function of graphics on your pages. Blind users using specially designed software will hear (via synthesized speech) the alternate messages you supply along with your graphics ("ALT" attributes in HTML) and so will not completely miss the content of your pictures and graphic navigation buttons. Users with text-only browsers or those who have turned off image display will see the alternate text in place of the visual content. If you use graphic menu systems for navigation, these text-based alternate menus are an especially important aid to users who cannot see your graphics (see Chapter 7, *Accessibility*). If you use graphics like single-pixel GIFs as spacers in your page layout, always be sure to include a blank ALT statement in the spacer image source tag (ALT=""). The blank ALT statement hides the graphic from text-only browsers and from browsers that read text aloud for visually impaired users:

```
<IMG SRC="pixel.gif" HEIGHT="1" WIDTH ="1" ALT="" HSPACE="5">
```

You should also include alternates as part of your page design for users who cannot access your primary content. For example, provide an equivalent text-only navigation menu for visually impaired users who cannot use your graphical menus. Or if you have video of a lecture or presentation on your site, include a text transcript or subtitles so that deaf users can have access to the materials.

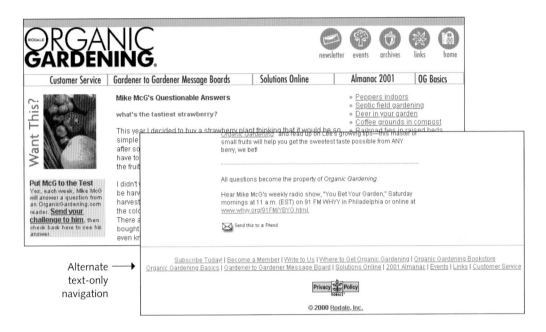

Alternate text-only navigation

Style sheets   Your content can be made more accessible if you use Cascading Style Sheets (CSS) to style your pages. With CSS-styled pages, users can easily apply personalized formatting to Web documents. A page designed using red text against a green background, for example, presents a problem for users with red-green color blindness: the contrast between text and background may not be great enough for the text to be distinguishable. If the colors are set via a style sheet, users can set their browser preferences to override your settings and can apply their own style sheet to the page instead. With CSS-styled pages, the user can transform Web content into a format that addresses their requirements for accessibility.

Accessibility guidelines   All professionally designed Web sites or intranet sites should meet at least the minimum standards for accessibility as defined by the World Wide Web Consortium guidelines. The W3C Web site contains extensive information on the details of how to make your site reasonably accessible to blind, deaf, or other disabled users (see below). Until recently Web designers faced difficulties in implementing many of the W3C accessibility suggestions because the most popular versions of the major Web browsers either did not implement newer technology standards like Cascading Style Sheets or implemented them inconsistently. Now that both Netscape Navigator 6 and Internet Explorer 5 are almost completely compatible with W3C standards, however, the reasons for not using CSS and other tools to increase the accessibility of Web information to disabled readers are disappearing.

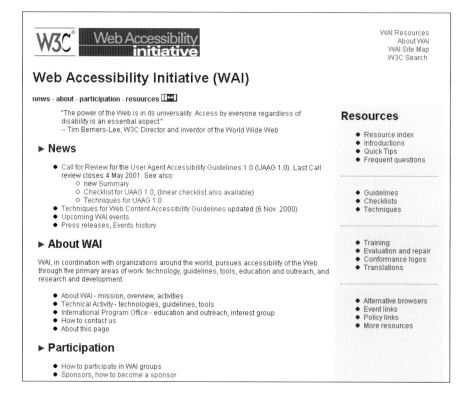

Graceful degradation We all hope that every reader will arrive using the latest version of a major Web browser and that their computers will be state-of-the-art models using fast connections to the Internet. The reality is almost always less than ideal. You don't need to design your Web site exclusively for the lowest common denominator of current computing and network technology, but you do need to consider what your site will look like to those readers who do not have the best equipment, current software, or good Internet connections. The problems here are aggravated by the fact that Web site developers generally have much better equipment than the average Web site reader. Don't design for *your* machine, design for your average reader.

Always check your page designs on typically sized display screens (800 × 600 pixels) to be sure that all major navigation and content areas fit well within the horizontal area of the screen. Usually that will limit your page layouts to no more than 760 pixels in width. Many users with slow modem connections routinely turn off the image display in their browser. Try turning off graphics in your Web browser and look at your pages—are they still intelligible and navigable? Do you use ALT statements for every graphic? Do you use blank ALT statements (ALT="") to hide irrelevant graphics or spacer graphics from text-only browsers?

Do not produce Web sites that depend on one browser technology or browser plug-in ("This site is optimized for Internet Explorer 5.5 and Macromedia Flash 5"). Such notes on the home page of a corporate or enterprise Web site look sophomoric and will drive away most adult users. Design for everyone using major browsers released in the two previous years. If you must depend on proprietary browser plug-ins, try to position the material that is dependent on the plug-in deeper within the site, where presumably the reader will already have made a commitment to your content and may not mind the bother of having to download a plug-in to see special features. Once readers have a clearer sense of what they might gain by bothering to download a browser plug-in, they can make an informed decision.

NAVIGATION

A rich set of graphic navigation and interactivity links within your Web pages will pull users' attention down the page, weaning them from the general-purpose browser links and drawing them further into your content. By providing your own consistent and predictable set of navigation buttons you also give the user a sense of your site's organization and make the logic and order of your site visually explicit. In this example the rich graphics and many links offered by the Salon technology and business page immediately draw the reader into the site:

Provide context or lose the reader   Readers need a sense of context, of their place within an organization of information. In paper documents this sense of "where you are" is a mixture of graphic and editorial organizational cues supplied by the graphic design of the book, the organization of the text, and the physical sensation of the book as an object. Electronic documents provide none of the physical cues we take for granted in assessing information. When we see a Web hypertext link on the page we have few cues to where we will be led, how much information is at the other end of the link, and exactly how the linked information relates to the current page. Even the view of individual Web pages is restricted for many users. Most Web pages don't fit completely on a standard office display monitor (800 × 600 pixels), and so there is almost always a part of the page that the user cannot see:

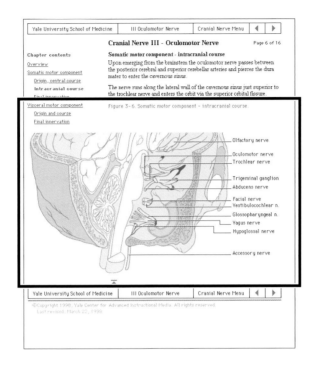

Web pages need to give the user explicit cues to the context and organization of information because only a small portion of any site (less than a page) is visible at one time:

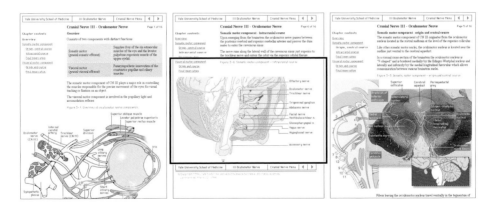

As the Web page designer it is up to you to provide these functional and context cues.

"Going back" and going to the previous page All hypertext systems share a common feature that has no direct precedent in print media: going "back" through a series of links you have previously visited is not the same as paging "back" through the preceding pages of an ordered sequence of pages. When users click on a hypertext link in a Web document they often are transported from one Web site to another, perhaps even from one country to another. Once made, the hypertext link is bidirectional; you can "go back" to the Web site you just left by clicking on the "Back" button of the viewer. Having hit the "Back" button, you can move to the new Web site again by hitting the "Forward" button:

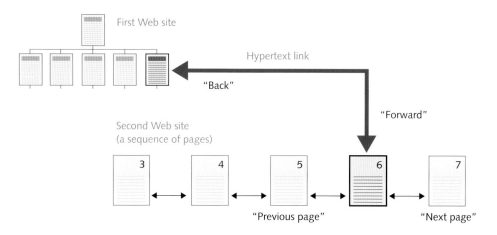

Button bars For the information designer hypertext links are a mixed blessing. The radical shifts in context that links create can easily confuse Web users, who need organized cues and interface elements if they are to follow and understand hypertext links from one Web page to another. This is particularly true when users need to be able to follow (or at least recognize) an ordered sequence of documents. Notice in the diagram above that although the user has entered the second Web site at page 6, the site is an ordered sequence of pages.

If the standard Web browser "Back" and "Forward" buttons are augmented with "Next Page" and "Previous Page" buttons built into the page, the user will have interface tools to navigate through the information in your site in the sequence you intended. Button bars can also display location information much as running chapter headers do in printed books:

Paging and location information

Paging buttons

Unlike the "Back" and "Forward" buttons, whose functions are relative only to the pages you have seen most recently, "Next Page" and "Previous Page" buttons in a document are fixed links you provide to associated documents. By providing paging buttons and links to local home pages and contents pages you give users the tools to understand how you have organized your Web site information, even if they have not entered your Web of pages through a home page or contents page. The buttons don't prevent people from reading the information in whatever order they choose, but they do allow readers to follow the sequence of pages you have laid out:

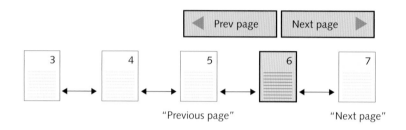

Button bars are also the most logical place for links back to your home page or to other menu pages related to the current page. A button bar can be built with text-based links or a series of individual button graphics at the top or bottom of the page:

REFERENCES

INTERFACE DESIGN AND THE WEB

Brewer, Judy, ed. 2001. *How people with disabilities use the Web.* http://www.w3c.org/WAI/EO/Drafts/PWD-Use-Web (31 March 2001).

Chisholm, Wendy, Gregg Vanderheiden, and Ian Jacobs, eds. 1999. *Web content accessibility guidelines 1.0.* http://www.w3c.org/TR/WAI-WEBCONTENT/wai-pageauth.html (17 January 2001).

Fleming, Jennifer. 1998. *Web navigation: Designing the user experience.* Sebastopol, Calif.: O'Reilly.

Krug, Steve. 2001. *Don't make me think! A common sense approach to Web usability.* Indianapolis, Ind.: Que.

McCloud, Scott. 1993. *Understanding comics: The invisible art.* New York: HarperCollins.

Nielsen, Jakob. 1995. *The alertbox: Current issues in Web usability.* http://www.useit.com/alertbox.

———. 1999. *Designing Web usability: The practice of simplicity.* Indianapolis, Ind.: New Riders.

Rosenfeld, Louis, and Peter Morville. 1998. *Information architecture for the World Wide Web.* Sebastopol, Calif.: O'Reilly.

University of Chicago Press. 1993. *The Chicago manual of style: The essential guide for writers, editors, and publishers,* 14th ed. Chicago: University of Chicago Press.

Veen, Jeffrey. 1997. *Hot Wired style: Principles for building smart Web sites.* San Francisco: Wired Books.

———. 2001. *The art and science of Web design.* Indianapolis, Ind.: New Riders.

Xerox Corporation. 1988. *Xerox publishing standards: A manual of style and design.* New York: Watson-Guptill.

HUMAN-COMPUTER INTERACTION

Apple Computer. 1992. *Macintosh human interface guidelines.* Reading, Mass.: Addison-Wesley.

Coe, Marlana. 1996. *Human factors for technical communicators.* New York: Wiley.

Mandel, T. 1997. *The elements of human interface design.* New York: Wiley.

Mullet, Kevin, and Darrell Sano. 1995. *Designing visual interfaces: Communication-oriented techniques.* Mountain View, Calif.: SunSoft.

Norman, Donald A. 1988. *The psychology of everyday things.* New York: Basic Books. [Now also published as *The design of everyday things.*]

3   *Site Design*

In architecture as in all other operative arts, the end must direct the
operation. The end is to build well. Well building hath three
conditions. Commodity, firmness, and delight.
—Sir Henry Wotton, *The Elements of Architecture*

THE DESIGN OF THE SITE will determine its organizational framework. At
this stage you will make the tactical design decisions about what your audience wants from you, what you wish to say, and how to arrange the content
to best meet your audience's needs. Although people will notice the graphic
design of your Web pages right away, the overall organization of the site will
have the greatest impact on their experience.

The fundamental organizing principle in Web site design is meeting
users' needs. Ask yourself what your audience wants, and center your site design on their needs. Many organizations and businesses make the mistake of
using their Web sites primarily to describe their administrative organization,
and only secondarily do they offer the services, products, and information
the average user is seeking. Most readers won't care how your company or
department is organized and will be put off if such inside information is all
your site appears to offer. Talk to the people who make up your target audience, put yourself in their shoes, and make the items and services they want
the most prominent items on the home page.

Notice, in the illustration below, how the major categories in the Yale–
New Haven Hospital home page center on the needs and interests of various audiences, not on how the hospital is organized:

ORGANIZING INFORMATION

Our day-to-day professional and social lives rarely demand that we create detailed architectures of what we know and how those structures of information are linked. Yet without a solid and logical organizational foundation, your Web site will not function well even if your basic content is accurate, attractive, and well written. Cognitive psychologists have known for decades that most people can hold only about four to seven discrete chunks of information in short-term memory. The way people seek and use reference information also suggests that smaller, discrete units of information are more functional and easier to handle than long, undifferentiated tracts.

There are five basic steps in organizing your information:

1 Divide your content into logical units
2 Establish a hierarchy of importance among the units
3 Use the hierarchy to structure relations among units
4 Build a site that closely follows your information structure
5 Analyze the functional and aesthetic success of your system

"CHUNKING" INFORMATION

Most information on the World Wide Web is gathered in short reference documents that are intended to be read nonsequentially. This is particularly true of sites whose contents are mostly technical or administrative documents. Long before the Web was invented, technical writers discovered that readers appreciate short "chunks" of information that can be located and scanned quickly. This method for presenting information translates well to the Web for several reasons:

- Few Web users spend time reading long passages of text on-screen. Most users either save long documents to disk or print them for more comfortable reading.
- Discrete chunks of information lend themselves to Web links. The user of a Web link usually expects to find a specific unit of relevant information, not a book's worth of general content. But don't overly subdivide your information or you will frustrate your readers. One to two pages (as printed) of information is about the maximum size for a discrete chunk of information on the Web.
- Chunking can help organize and present information in a uniform format. This allows users not only to apply past experience with a site to future searches and explorations but also to predict how an unfamiliar section of a Web site will be organized.
- Concise chunks of information are better suited to the computer screen, which provides a limited view of long documents. Long Web pages tend to disorient readers; they require users to scroll long distances and to remember what is off-screen.

The concept of a chunk of information must be flexible and consistent with common sense, logical organization, and convenience. Let the nature of the content suggest how it should be subdivided and organized. At times it makes sense to provide long documents as a subdivided and linked set of Web pages. Although short Web documents are usually preferable, it often makes little sense to divide a long document arbitrarily, particularly if you want users to be able to print easily or save the entire document in one step.

Hierarchy of importance   Hierarchical organization is virtually a necessity on the Web. Most sites depend on hierarchies, moving from the most general overview of the site (the home page), down through increasingly specific submenus and content pages. Chunks of information should be ranked in importance and organized by the interrelations among units. Once you have determined a logical set of priorities, you can build a hierarchy from the most important or general concepts down to the most specific or detailed topics.

Relations   When confronted with a new and complex information system, users build mental models. They use these models to assess relations among topics and to guess where to find things they haven't seen before. The success of the organization of your Web site will be determined largely by how well your system matches your users' expectations. A logical site organization allows users to make successful predictions about where to find things. Consistent methods of displaying information permit users to extend their knowledge from familiar pages to unfamiliar ones. If you mislead users with a structure that is neither logical nor predictable, they will be frustrated by the difficulties of getting around. You don't want your users' mental model of your Web site to look like this:

Function   Once you have created your site, analyze its functionality. Efficient Web site design is largely a matter of balancing the relation of menu, or home, pages with individual content pages. The goal is to build a hierarchy of menus and pages that feels natural to users and doesn't mislead them or interfere with their use of the site.

Web sites with too shallow a hierarchy depend on massive menu pages that can degenerate into a confusing "laundry list" of unrelated information:

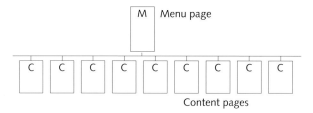

Menu schemes can also be too deep, burying information beneath too many layers of menus. Having to navigate through layers of nested menus before reaching real content is frustrating:

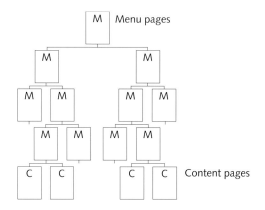

If your Web site is actively growing, the proper balance of menus and content pages is a moving target. Feedback from users (and analyzing your own use of the site) can help you decide if your menu scheme has outlived its usefulness or has weak areas. Complex document structures require deeper menu hierarchies, but users should never be forced into page after page of menus if direct access is possible. With a well-balanced, functional hierarchy you can offer users menus that provide quick access to information and reflect the organization of your site.

SUMMARY

The most important step in planning your site is to organize your information. Thinking carefully about what you want to say and how you want to say it requires that you become intimately acquainted with your site content. Create outlines, chunk your information into sections and subsections, think about how the sections relate to one another, and create a table of contents. This exercise will help immensely when it comes time to build the individual pages of your site and may determine the eventual success of your Web site.

A well-organized table of contents can be a major navigation tool in your Web site. The table is more than a list of links—it gives the user an overview of the organization, extent, and narrative flow of your presentation:

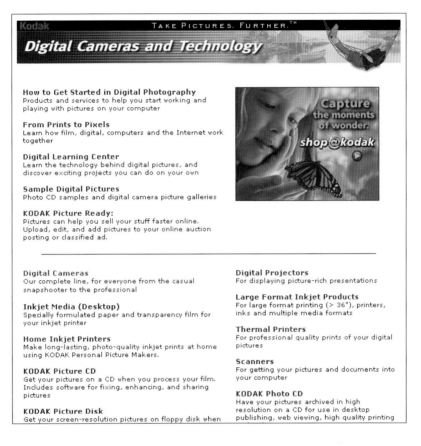

SITE STRUCTURE

If you are interested in the World Wide Web you can hardly escape references to hypertext and hypermedia. The computer press is full of fuzzy thinking about how Web-based information can somehow "link everything to everything." The implication is that with the Web you can dispense with one of the most challenging aspects of presenting information—putting it into a logical order and creating an interesting and understandable resource for readers. But if your idea of how one section of your site relates to other areas is hazy, if you have no comprehensive narrative or clear sense of organization, your readers will know it soon enough, and most will leave in pursuit of material that is better organized.

Web sites are built around basic structural themes. These fundamental architectures govern the navigational interface of the Web site and mold the user's mental models of how the information is organized. Three essential structures can be used to build a Web site: sequences, hierarchies, and webs.

Sequences   The simplest way to organize information is to place it in a sequence. Sequential ordering may be chronological, a logical series of topics progressing from the general to the specific, or alphabetical, as in indexes, encyclopedias, and glossaries. Straight sequences are the most appropriate organization for training sites, for example, in which the reader is expected to go through a fixed set of material and the only links are those that support the linear navigation path:

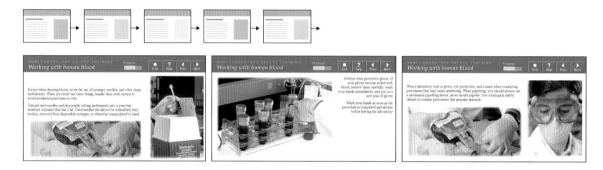

More complex Web sites may still be organized as a logical sequence, but each page in the main sequence may have links to one or more pages of digressions, parenthetical information, or information on other Web sites:

Hierarchies   Information hierarchies are the best way to organize most complex bodies of information. Because Web sites are usually organized around a single home page, hierarchical schemes are particularly suited to Web site organization. Hierarchical diagrams are very familiar in corporate and institutional life, so most users find this structure easy to understand. A hierarchical organization also imposes a useful discipline on your own analytical approach to your content, because hierarchies are practical only with well-organized material.

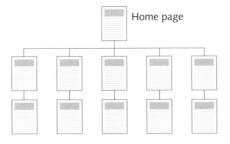

Home page

Webs Weblike organizational structures pose few restrictions on the pattern of information use. In this structure the goal is often to mimic associative thought and the free flow of ideas, allowing users to follow their interests in a unique, heuristic, idiosyncratic pattern. This organizational pattern develops with dense links both to information elsewhere in the site and to information at other sites. Although the goal of this organization is to exploit the Web's power of linkage and association to the fullest, weblike structures can just as easily propagate confusion. Ironically, associative organizational schemes are often the most impractical structure for Web sites because they are so hard for the user to understand and predict. Webs work best for small sites dominated by lists of links and for sites aimed at highly educated or experienced users looking for further education or enrichment and not for a basic understanding of a topic.

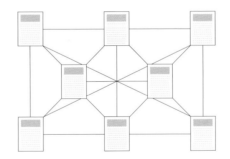

CREATING SITE DIAGRAMS

Site planning with a team is often easier if you base your major structural planning and decisions on a shared master site diagram that all members of the group can work with. The site diagram should evolve as the plan evolves and can act as the core planning document as changes are proposed and made in the diagram. Site diagrams are excellent for planning both the broad scope of the site and the details of where each piece of content, navigation, or interactive functionality will appear. In well-equipped Web projects the team meetings often center on a computer and data projector showing Web pages or PowerPoint graphics. Although there is no substitute for looking at actual Web pages, ironically, this reliance on data projection is a severe limitation in explaining complex Web site structures to a team. No matter how good your data projector is, you can show only one Web page at a time in a Web browser, and no current data projector can match the resolution, size, or flexibility (you can write on it) of a large paper diagram. For major planning meetings we often print at least one very large color diagram of the site organization, so that everyone can see the "big picture" as it develops from meeting to meeting. The site diagram dominates the middle of the conference table, becoming a tactile, malleable representation of the plan as it evolves. Everyone is free to make notes on it or suggest improvements in the site structure, and the revised diagram becomes the official result of the meeting.

Site file and directory structures   Site diagrams are also useful when your project moves from planning to actual Web page production. As the new site is built up in a directory on the Web server, the site diagram is often the first place programmers look to gain an understanding of how the site files should be subdivided into directories ("folders") on the server.

The pattern of directories and subdirectories of the site files should mirror the major content divisions and structures as shown on the site diagram:

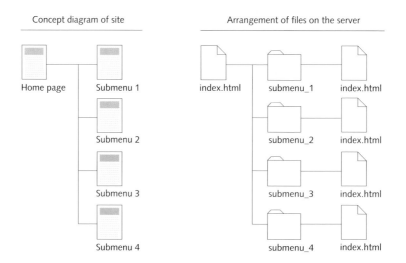

As the site directories and subdirectories are organized on the server, information on the exact names used for major directories and files should be added to the site diagram, so that everyone on the team has a ready current reference to the naming conventions and file locations in the site.

SUMMARY

Most complex Web sites share aspects of all three types of information structures. Except in sites that rigorously enforce a sequence of pages, users are likely to use your site in a free-form weblike manner, just as they would a reference book. But the nonlinear usage patterns typical of Web surfers do not absolve you of the need to organize your thinking and present it within a clear, consistent structure that complements your design goals. The chart below summarizes the three basic organization patterns against the "linearity" of the narrative and the complexity of the content:

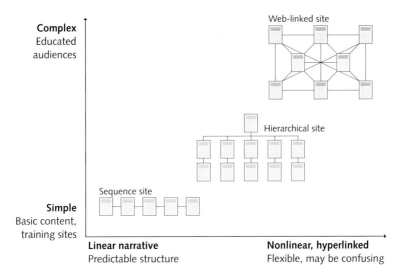

SITE DESIGN THEMES

All presentations of information are governed by parameters determined by the objectives, the practical logistics of the chosen medium, and the audience. The figure below plots major themes for information delivery against two fundamental variables—the linearity of the structure of your presentation and the length of the typical user's contact time:

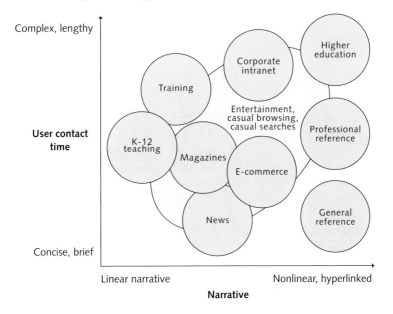

Some general modes of Web use are more structured and depend on audiences who arrive knowing what they wish to accomplish without the need for site-supplied motivation. Corporate intranets, training sites, educational sites, reference sites, and many well-known news and information sites benefit from audiences that know what to expect at a particular site and arrive there with a specific goal in mind. E-commerce and entertainment sites have a complex dual mission to balance: to motivate casual browsers to spend time in the site and become customers as well as to provide fast access to products and information to experienced users.

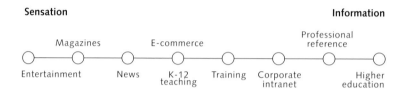

Naive designers and clients eager to do almost anything to attract attention to a Web site consistently make the mistake of maximizing immediate graphic impact over all other possible attributes of a site design. They have the misguided notion that if you constantly hit the reader between the eyes with a huge, noisy graphic or Flash animation, you will sustain their attention. Sometimes this does work—for about ten to fifteen seconds. "Eye candy" is a quick blast of visual sweets, but you can't build a Web site on a moment's attention. Most readers quickly tire of blaring animated graphics and the long downloads, plug-in compatibility irritations, and distracting stimuli that complicate such sites. A successful site requires real, sustained engagement, and you get that only by offering both sophisticated visual stimuli and a site that is structured to meet the needs of its audience quickly and effectively.

Training Web-based training applications tend to be linear in design and typically present few opportunities to digress from the central flow of the presentation. Don't confuse readers or confound your own expectations by offering many links away from the central message. Restricting links to the "Next" and "Previous" paging functions guarantees that everyone will see the same core presentation and allows you to predict users' contact time more accurately. Most training presentations assume a contact time of less than one hour or are broken up into sessions of an hour or less. Tell your readers how long the session will last, and warn them not to digress from the required material if they are to receive credit for the training. Training applications typically require a user log-in and often present forms-based quiz questions in true-false or multiple-choice formats. User registration data and scores are typically stored in a database linked to the Web site.

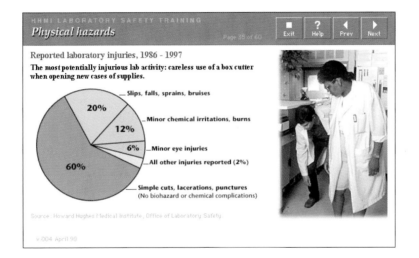

Teaching   Good teaching applications are also built around a strong central narrative, but they typically offer more opportunities to pursue interesting digressions from the main themes of the Web site. The information presented is usually more sophisticated and in-depth than in training applications. Links are the most powerful aspect of the Web, but they can also be a distraction that may prevent visitors from getting through the presentation. If you wish to provide links to other Web-based resources beyond your local site, you might consider grouping the links on a separate page away from the main body of the material. Often readers will want to print material from a teaching site and read it later from paper. Make this easy for them by providing a "printing" version that consolidates many separate pages into one long page.

ChemLab

| Info | Techniques | Chem 3/5 | Chem 6 |

Glassware
Burets
Flasks, Beakers, & Graduated Cylinders
Pipets
Repipets
Volumetric Flasks

Instruments
Analytical Balance
pH Meter: Analog
pH Meter: Digital
Spectrometer: Analog
Spectrometer: Digital
Spectrometer: Scanning
Top-loading Balance

Techniques
Calorimetry
Centrifugation
Quantitative Transfer
Titration
Vacuum Filtration

ChemLab Home

Buret

A buret is used to deliver solution in precisely-measured, variable volumes. They are used primarily for titration, to deliver one reactant until the precise end point of the reaction is reached.

Using a Buret

To fill a buret, close the stopcock at the bottom and use a funnel. You may need to lift up on the funnel slightly, to allow the solution to flow in freely.

You can also fill a buret using a disposable transfer pipet. This works better than a funnel for the small, 10 mL burets. Be sure the transfer pipet is dry or conditioned with the titrant, so the concentration of solution will not be changed.

Before titrating, conditon the buret with titrant solution and check that the buret is flowing freely. To condition a piece of glassware, rinse it so that all surfaces are coated with solution, then drain. Conditioning two or three times will insure that the concentration of titrant is not changed by a stray drop of water.

Continuing education   The audiences for heuristic, self-directed learning will chafe at design strategies that are too restrictive or linear. The typical corporate or academic user of such sites is usually fairly knowledgeable in the subject area. The Web is an ideal medium for "just in time" training, where users pick just the specific topic where they need education. Flexible, interactive, nonlinear design structures are ideal for these readers because it is difficult to predict exactly which topics will most interest them. The design must permit fast access to a wide range of topics and is typically dense with links to related material within the local site and beyond on the World Wide Web. Text-based lists of links work well here for tables of contents and indexes because they load fast and are full of information, but well-designed graphics and illustrations are also needed so that this easily bored audience will stay involved with the material. Contact times are unpredictable but are often shorter than for training or teaching sites because the readers are usually under time pressure. Easy printing options are another must for this audience.

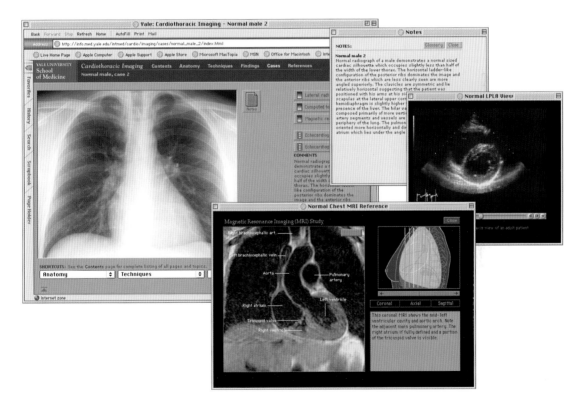

Reference   The best-designed reference Web sites allow readers to pop into the site, find what they want, and easily print or download what they find. There is typically no "story" to tell, so usage patterns are nonlinear. Non-essential graphics should be minimal and undistracting, and content and menu structure must be carefully organized to support fast search and retrieval, easy downloading of files, and convenient printing options. A well-designed search engine is a must for sites with more than thirty pages, or sites that store long text documents in single Web pages. You may wish to investigate more sophisticated multiparameter search software instead of relying on single keyword searches. Contact time is typically brief in reference sites: the shorter the better.

Entertainment and magazine sites Unlike the sites covered thus far, entertainment sites usually cater to an audience whose interests and motivations are usually much less focused. This audience needs to be grabbed immediately by compelling graphic and text presentations, or they'll simply hop somewhere else in search of stimulation. As in any other design genre, what is "compelling" depends entirely on the audience's expectations. Slate's sophisticated mix of political commentary and social criticism depends heavily on clever, well-written headlines and teasers. The well-designed home page presentation is derived entirely from presentation styles used in political and current affairs magazines, because that's exactly the audience Slate is seeking.

Unfortunately, content presentation in entertainment and magazine sites is consistently marred by the intrusion of banner ads, whose winking, blinking, and blaring colored boxes interfere with on-screen reading.

News sites News sites have largely adapted the existing design genres of print newspapers and magazines to the smaller format of the Web. Virtually all of the design conventions used on the *New York Times* Web site derive from well-established print precedents, although ironically, the *New York Times's* louder, more colorful Web presence owes more to the exaggerated visual hierarchies of *USA Today* than to the *Times's* conservative print conventions.

Fortunately, aside from the newspapers themselves, there are excellent resources available for learning the conventions and terminology of journalistic graphic design. Tim Harrower's *Newspaper Designer's Handbook* and other similar books are filled with useful presentation devices that translate easily to a Web page and have the additional benefit of being familiar to the news audience.

E-commerce   In e-commerce sites the crucial design parameters are efficient navigation and search, along with speed to the final "place order" button. During the "dot-com" market bubble many new e-commerce sites spent fortunes of their investors' money on elaborate Macromedia Flash or digital video presentations and quickly failed—some went bankrupt before the site was launched. Meanwhile, the Web's most successful commerce sites kept things technically simple and basic. Amazon, eBay, Yahoo!, and other successful Web commerce sites use remarkably spare page design schemes and simple text- or tab-based navigation systems. Another area where e-commerce sites often fail is in providing search engines that are smart enough to "degrade gracefully" when there is no exact match to a request. If a shopper types in "PDA" and the inventory fails to turn up any products by that exact name, the search engine should default to a list of "personal digital assistants" made by various manufacturers.

Search results for "pda"

Amazon has experimented with various tab systems as the site has grown, but the choice of tabs as a navigation system was wise—tabs are one of the few real-world graphic navigation metaphors to have translated to the screen. Tabs work with only about eight or fewer choices, however. As tabs multiply, their sheer number creates confusion.

Amazon's order processing screens are also a model of navigation design for Web commerce. Most well-designed order screens are short and deal with topics one at a time (review items in "shopping cart," provide shipping address, add credit card information, and so on) on screens that don't require scrolling. But this forces the order process to take place over multiple screens, which could become tedious if not for the "you are here" progress icons at the top of the screen. The lesson here is clear: all e-commerce processes involve some tedium for the buyer. Yet if you provide information on the user's current position, the slow series of screens becomes less of a problem because the user knows what to expect.

Progress icons tell you where you are in the process, and where you still have to go

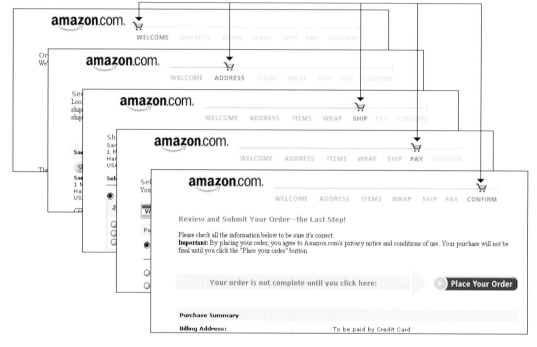

SITE ELEMENTS

Web sites vary enormously in their style, content, organization, and purpose, but all Web sites that are designed primarily to act as information resources share certain characteristics.

HOME PAGES

All Web sites are organized around a home page that acts as a logical point of entry into the system of Web pages in a site. In hierarchical organizations, the home page sits at the top of the chart, and all pages in the Web site should contain a direct link back to the home page. The World Wide Web URL for a home page is the Web "address" that points users to the Web site. In many cases, home page addresses are used more than home and business street addresses.

The thirty square inches at the top of a home page comprise the most visible area of the Web site. Most readers will be looking at your site on a seventeen- to nineteen-inch monitor, and the top four or five vertical inches are all that is sure to be visible on their screens. The best visual metaphor here is to a newspaper page—position matters. It's nice to be on the front page, but stories "above the fold" are much more visible than those below. In sites designed for efficient navigation the density of links at the top of the home page should be maximal—you'll never get a better chance to offer your readers exactly what they want in the first page they see:

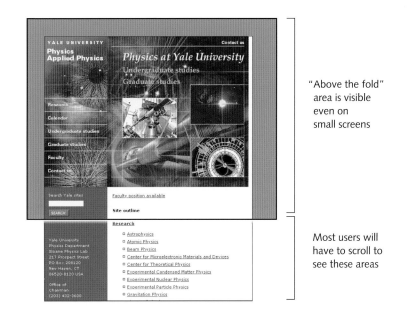

"Above the fold" area is visible even on small screens

Most users will have to scroll to see these areas

Home pages perform a variety of functions. Some designs primarily take advantage of the high visibility of the home page; it's the most visited page of your site and is therefore ideal for posting news and information. The high visibility of the home page also makes it the ideal place to put a menu of links or table of contents for the site. Navigation schemes in sites that use the home page for news and menu listings are often centered on the home page, using it as the "home base" for most navigation through the site. Other home page designs use the home page as the first opportunity to steer audiences into subtopic or special interest areas of the site. The following are the most common home page design strategies:

Menu home pages   Menu-like lists of links dominated the design of most home pages in the first few years of the Web, and this remains the most common type of home page. Menu-style pages need not be dominated by plain lists of text-based HTML links—graphic imagemaps are often more space efficient, packing the maximal number of links into every square inch of the page. Sophisticated designs combine graphic imagemaps and blocks of text-based links. Text links offer less visual impact but are much easier to change on short notice.

News-oriented home pages   The home pages of such organizations as the *New York Times* and cnn (Cable News Network) are obvious examples here, but many organizations take advantage of the high visibility of their home pages to make announcements to both employees and the larger Web audience. Live information makes a home page more attractive and more likely to generate repeat visits. Many home page designs reserve one or more areas for late-breaking news, calendar events, or alert messages. If you choose this approach, standardize the location and nature of the news areas within a general page framework that remains stable over time. Readers will be disoriented if your home page changes too much from week to week.

Path-based home pages   Large Web sites offer so much information to so many audiences that it can be impossible to represent the depth and breadth of the site content in a single home page. In addition, readers often come to a Web site with specific interests or goals in mind. In such cases it is often advantageous to use the home page to split the audience immediately into interest groups and to offer them specific, more relevant information in menu pages deeper within the site.

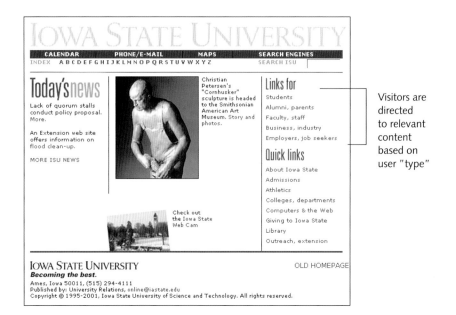

Visitors are directed to relevant content based on user "type"

Splash screens Splash screens, or site covers, are the most controversial of all site elements. For many readers, site covers are simply an additional and annoying mouse click between them and the content they are seeking. Such readers would like to be presented with a site index at the start rather than a splash screen with pretty graphics or spiffy animations. The key is to assess your audience and then choose the entry that seems most appropriate.

Consider the function of your site. Is your typical visitor there for a single visit or will they visit often? An online tool such as a calendar or search engine should not have a purely aesthetic site cover, because visitors may visit the site several times a day. An elegant but nonfunctional cover on such a site will soon become tedious. Of course, visitors who do not wish to enter through the front door can simply bookmark an internal page of your site, such as the table of contents. But if you find yourself repeatedly making this argument *for* using a splash screen, you may wish to adapt or even remove your cover to better accommodate your audience.

The success of splash screens depends enormously on the expectations of the site visitor. If you were to visit a site about a poet you would enter with different expectations than you would when visiting a site about carpal tunnel syndrome. Visitors to a site about poetry may not simply be out Web foraging but may instead be looking for an experience, for art, for entertainment. A mysterious, enigmatic, aesthetically pleasing facade might just entice such visitors in.

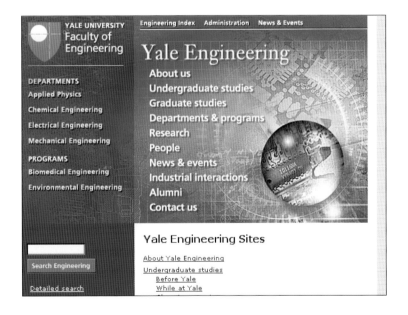

One of these four basic schemes may dominate the home page design, but increasingly home pages are a complex amalgam of all strategies. The Library of Congress's THOMAS home page mixes images, menu lists, and special interest sections:

THOMAS
Legislative Information on the Internet

In the Spirit of
Thomas Jefferson,
a service of
The Library of Congress

House Floor This Week | House Floor Now | Senate Schedule

Search Bill Text for 107th Congress (2001-2002)
By Bill Number [ ]   By Word/Phrase [ ]   [Search] [Clear]
For previous Congress, select Bill Text (below) and then select 106.

What's New in THOMAS?

Frequently Asked Questions (FAQ)

107th Congress:
House Directories
Senate Directories

Congressional
Internet Services:
House · Senate
Library of Congress
GPO · GAO · CBO
AOC · OTA

Library of Congress
Web Links:
Legislative NEW
Executive
Judicial
State/Local

The Legislative Process:
House
Senate
Summary of Congressional Activity

Historical Documents

LEGISLATION

Bill Summary & Status
93rd - 107th

Bill Text
101st - 107th

Public Laws By Law Number
93rd - 107th

CONGRESSIONAL RECORD

Most Recent Issue

Text Search
101st - 107th

Index
104th - 107th

Roll Call Votes:
House
Senate

COMMITTEE INFORMATION

Committee Reports
104th - 107th

House Committees:
Home Pages, Schedules, and Hearings

Senate Committees:
Home Pages, Schedules, and Hearings

Legislation Related to the Attack of September 11, 2001 NEW

Status of FY2002 Appropriations Bills

Status of FY2001 Appropriations Bills

Consolidated Appropriations Act for FY2001 Conference Report

Consolidated Appropriations Act for FY2000 Conference Report

National Bipartisan Commission on the Future of Medicare.

H.R. 4328 The Omnibus Appropriations Bill for FY 1999.

FirstGov.gov: Comprehensive links to U.S. Government websites.

Graphics or text?   The primary layout decision you will make about your home page is how heavily you will use graphics on the page. Most corporate, institutional, and education home pages display at least a small graphic banner across the top of the home page, and in commercial sites the trend is rapidly moving toward complex mixtures of links embedded in graphic imagemaps and links in text that emulate the look and functions of CD-ROM multimedia title pages or print magazines. Although strong graphics can be effective at grabbing a browser's attention, large graphic menus impose long loading times for pages, especially for users linking to the Internet via modems or slow network connections. Even if the user is accessing your Web site at Ethernet speeds, graphic menus may still load many times slower than text-based lists of links.

This dichotomy between slow-loading but attractive graphics-based home pages and fast-loading but prosaic text-based home pages also reflects the need to address multiple audiences with different expectations. The goals for most Web sites are to transmit internal information (to students, employees, and clients) and to communicate with potential clients and the general Web-browsing public. The Guggenheim Museum has opted for a graphic home page design, but the layout is carefully designed to stay within the dimensions of the average office monitor. Because the graphic area is moderately sized, the page loads reasonably quickly for a graphic menu:

The relatively plain, mostly text-based home page for the World Wide Web Consortium offers an efficient ratio of links per kilobyte of page size, but at some cost in pure visual appeal. The page is fast-loading and well-designed for its audience of Web specialists but would not attract the average browser through presentation alone:

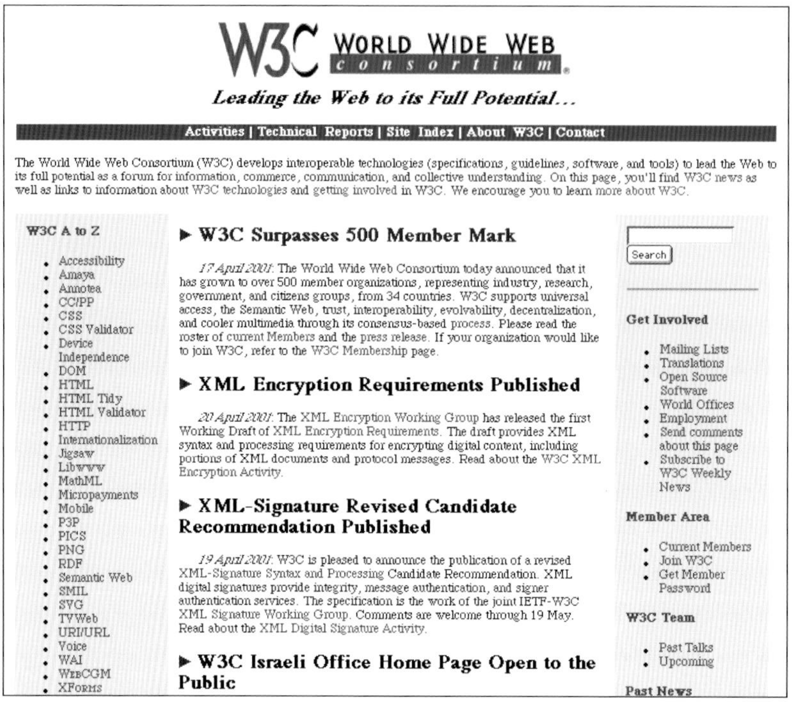

The best way to meet the needs of both casual browsers and highly targeted frequent users is to present alternative views of your Web site. One approach is to make a visually attractive main home page aimed at the general audience of Web browsers but also to offer a more text-oriented alternate home page that emphasizes rapid access to information via detailed text menus. Another approach is to use a graphic banner at the top of the home page, followed by a set of text-based links. The home page for *The Atlantic Online* reflects this dual approach, with a moderate-sized graphic image topping a well-organized set of text links:

Many Web users who access the Internet via modems choose not to load graphics and thus will not see menu links embedded in imagemap graphics. If you choose to depend on links embedded in imagemaps, it is crucial to provide alternative text-based links that will remain visible even if readers have chosen to turn off the display of graphics. Many sites provide these text-based links in small sizes below the page footer, where they are accessible but do not disrupt the overall design of the page:

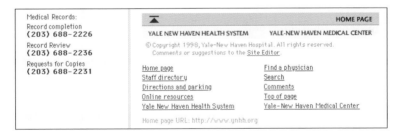

The master page layout grid   The home page usually gets the most attention in the beginning of a Web site design project. Your home page is important, but remember—it is inherently singular. Don't let the design of the home page dominate your site design strategies. When designing a large Web site it's much more important to concentrate on the standard layout grid that all the internal pages of the site will share. After all, you'll have only one home page, but you could easily have thousands of internal pages as the site grows. If you make a mistake on the home page you only have one page to fix. If you make a mistake in creating the basic internal page grid you could soon have thousands of pages to fix. The overall success of the Web site will depend more on a strong, logical page grid than on the appeal of the site's home page. The details of page layout grids are discussed in the following chapters, but we raise the issue of page grids here because it is a crucial design decision when creating a Web site. Think about it: if you tire of your home page, you have only one page to change. Make a big mistake with your page grid and you could end up with thousands of poorly designed pages.

Constructing a layout grid usually begins by analyzing the content structure you have worked out and deciding what (besides the all-important home page link) you will need for the most general navigation purposes. Here you are trying to establish what links will be present and generally useful on every page of your Web site. If you work in a corporation or any sizeable government or nonprofit enterprise you must also consider how your particular site fits into the larger context of the other Web sites in your enterprise. Does your enterprise already have an established and successful Web design format that you can adopt? If not, carefully consider what links, logos, and other graphic and functional elements reflecting your place in the larger enterprise should be present on all of your pages. The goal is to establish a logical and consistent approach to where basic graphic identity elements, navigation links, and other essential information appear on every page within your site. Terminology is also crucial here: choose your words carefully for links and titles, and solicit comments and feedback from fellow team members and site users. A misleading or confusing label or phrase can ruin the functionality of a link.

A page grid establishes the number, location, and terminology of all major page links and page graphic elements:

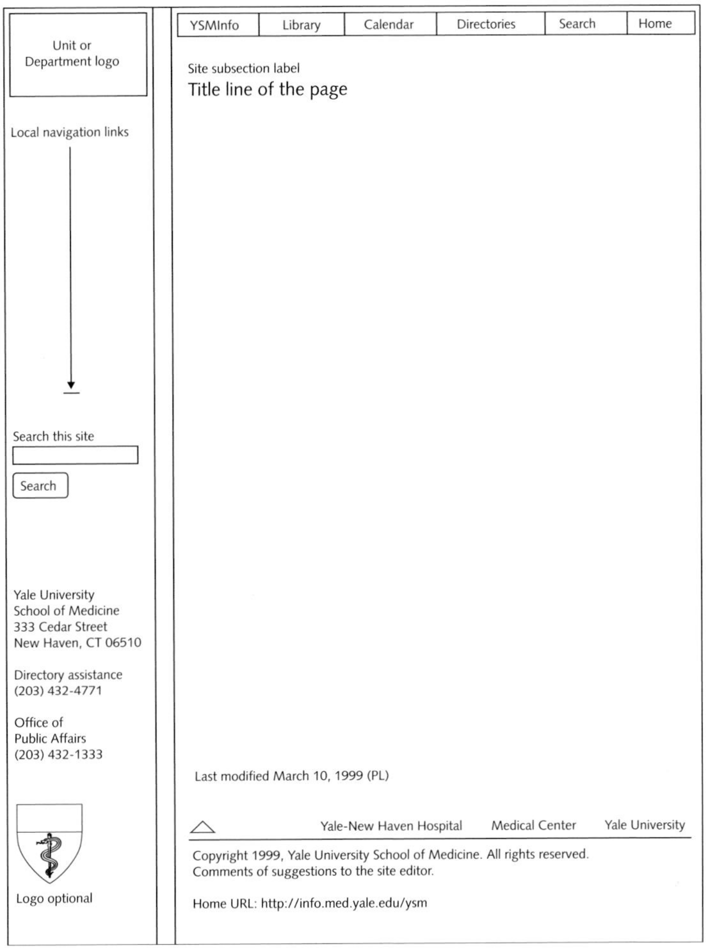

YSMInfo	Library	Calendar	Directories	Search	Home

Unit or
Department logo

Site subsection label
Title line of the page

Local navigation links

Search this site

Search

Yale University
School of Medicine
333 Cedar Street
New Haven, CT 06510

Directory assistance
(203) 432-4771

Office of
Public Affairs
(203) 432-1333

Last modified March 10, 1999 (PL)

Yale-New Haven Hospital   Medical Center   Yale University

Copyright 1999, Yale University School of Medicine. All rights reserved.
Comments of suggestions to the site editor.

Logo optional

Home URL: http://info.med.yale.edu/ysm

Note that so far we have not discussed specific graphic elements in relation to the page grid. A page grid can be used to enforce a very rigid, visually consistent identity scheme by incorporating information on the exact graphics, logos, fonts, colors, and wording of page elements:

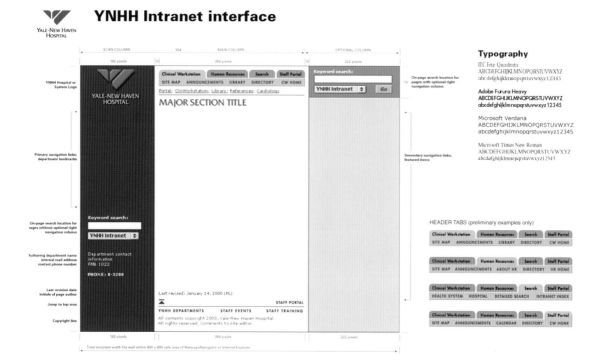

However, a page grid is also a great way to allow a variety of visual approaches to site design within an enterprise while maintaining a reasonably consistent navigational interface for the user. All three of these pages, though they use a variety of colors and graphic schemes, share the same underlying page grid that specifies the position and wording of major navigation links and other page elements:

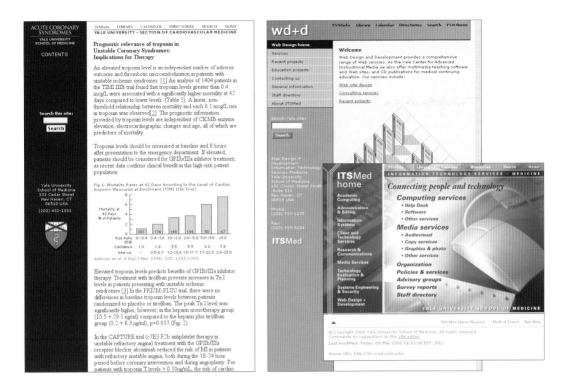

After establishing the internal page grid you can build the site home page on the same underlying grid, so that readers who come to your site are immediately introduced to the page grid, identity graphics, and navigation scheme that is used throughout the site. The home page grid does not have to be identical to the internal page grid; home pages must provide a much wider range of content and navigation elements than the average internal page. For this reason home pages are often much wider to fill the screen and more graphic than the average internal page:

Home page

Internal page

MENUS AND SUBSITES

Unless your site is small you will probably need a number of submenu pages that users enter from a general category listing on your home page. In complex sites with multiple topic areas it is not practical to burden the home page with dozens of links—the page grows too long to load in a timely manner, and its sheer complexity may be off-putting to many users. Providing a submenu page for each topic will create a mini-home page for each section of the site. For specialized, detailed submenus you could even encourage frequent users to link there directly. In this way the submenus will become alternate home pages in "subsites" oriented to a specific audience. Be sure to include a basic set of links to other sections of the site on each subsite home page, and always include a link back to your main organization home page.

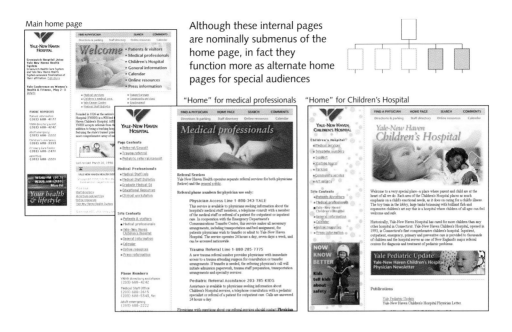

Main home page

Although these internal pages are nominally submenus of the home page, in fact they function more as alternate home pages for special audiences

"Home" for medical professionals   "Home" for Children's Hospital

RESOURCE LISTS, "OTHER RELATED SITES" PAGES

The World Wide Web is growing so rapidly that even the large commercial Web index services such as Yahoo! and Excite are only partial listings of the information accessible through the Web. When authors begin to build Web sites, their first page is often a collection of favorite links to sites related to their profession, industry, or interests. In a corporate or institutional site, a well-edited, well-maintained "Other useful sites" page may be the most valuable and heavily used resource.

SITE GUIDES

Unlike print media, where the physical heft and dimensions of a book or magazine give instant cues to the amount of information to expect, Web sites often give few explicit indications of the depth and extent of the content available. This is especially true when the home page does not provide an extensive listing of internal site links. Although search facilities offer users quick access to your content, they are no substitute for a clear, well-organized exposition of your site's contents. Even the best search engines are relatively stupid and have only the most primitive means of assessing the priority, relevance, and interrelations of the information resources you offer in your Web site.

Tables of contents or site indexes   Tables of contents and keyword indexes of the information in your Web site are an easy way to give readers a clear sense of the extent, organization, and context of your site content. Tables of contents and indexes are familiar print conventions; readers understand them and will appreciate the overviews, perspectives, and efficient navigation they afford. The main difference between Web-based indexes and their print counterparts is that a Web site index need not be as extensive or detailed as a book index because you can always use a search engine to find every obscure reference to a keyword. A Web site index should point to the most relevant and useful occurrences of a keyword and ignore minor references (those will turn up in a keyword search anyway).

Site maps Site maps give the reader an overview of the site contents. Site maps come in two varieties: graphic diagrams that literally use the "map" metaphor and organized list links to major pages within the site.

The form of graphic site maps varies from hierarchical branching diagrams to geographic metaphors, but they all share the same limitations:

- Graphic maps of large or complex Web sites are at best simple metaphors that convey only the approximate outlines of the site content. Computer screens offer limited space, so site map graphics tend to oversimplify and exaggerate hierarchies of information. The results are seldom worth the time and expense involved in making the graphic, unless you mean to convey only the broadest outlines of the site structure. Unless your Web site deals with information that is inherently spatial (a set of maps, for instance), text-based tables of contents or indexes will always be more efficient and informative.
- Graphic site maps are often complex graphic files, which are harder to change as your site evolves.
- Graphic site maps are inherently large graphics and are slow to download.

Site maps based on carefully organized text links of major menus and sub-menu pages and major page titles are much more informative than graphic maps and can easily be updated as your site matures. Most effective text site maps are really just expanded tables of contents. As such they are instantly familiar and understood by the vast majority of the readers in your audience. Bitstream's site map is a particularly well designed example of this type:

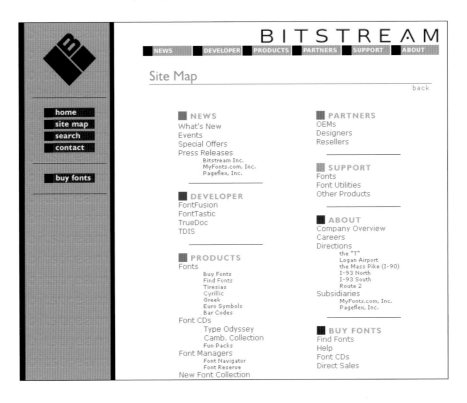

"WHAT'S NEW?" PAGES

Many Web sites need to be updated frequently so that the information they present doesn't become stale. But the presence of new information may not be obvious to readers unless you make a systematic effort to inform them. If items that appear on your home page menu are updated, you could place a "new" graphic next to each updated item. If, however, your site is complex, with many levels of information spread over dozens (or hundreds) of pages, you might consider making a "What's New" page designed specifically to inform users of updated information throughout the site.

Every Web page in a corporate or institutional site should carry a revision date that is changed each time the page is updated so that users can be sure they have the latest version. Many readers print pages from the Web. Without a revision date, your readers have no way of telling whether the page they printed is current or outdated.

Search facilities are a necessity for large sites and are convenient even for smaller sites that contain long documents. Sites that are updated frequently also require a good search engine, because your menus and site index will probably not keep pace with every change you make in the content pages of the site. But search engines are no substitute for a carefully organized browsing structure of menus and submenus. The two systems, browsing by menu and searching by keyword, complement each other—neither system alone is adequate. Keyword searches give the reader specific links to follow but with no overview of the nature and extent of your content and no feel for how you have organized the information. Menus and tables of contents are great for broad overviews, but if your readers are looking for a specific piece of information not mentioned in the contents, they may miss what you have to offer.

The search software you use will often dictate the user interface for searching. If you update your content frequently, be sure that your search engine's indexing is done at least daily. Also be sure that your readers understand exactly what content is being searched: the entire Web site or just a subsection? If your site is complex you may wish to offer readers a pop-up menu that lists the areas of your site and allows them to limit their search to a specific area. And make sure that the results page also matches the graphic design of the site.

The Web is a bidirectional medium—people expect to be able to send you comments, questions, and suggestions. Always provide at least one link to an email address in a prominent location in your site. You can request user information and feedback using Web page forms and then use a database to store and analyze their input.

The logistical and support staff implications of creating a popular Web site are often overlooked until a crisis develops. Rolling out a new, heavily trafficked Web site is like suddenly adding a second front door to your enterprise. Who will greet the people who come flooding in? Who will answer their questions about your organization and its products and services? Who will collect and analyze the information you receive from your readers? Before you add this functionality to your Web pages, be sure you have an infrastructure in place to handle the fruits of your success.

Street addresses, phone numbers, fax numbers   It is amazing how often site developers forget that not all communication with the organization goes through the Web site. Even if you have a great Web site, people will still want to call you, send you mail and express packages, and fax you documents. Your home page should include the same contact information you provide on your stationery, marketing materials, and business cards. If your home page design doesn't allow adequate space for this information, at least provide a link to another page with contact information.

Maps, travel directions, parking information Your Web site is an ideal place to make travel information available to clients, visitors, vendors—anyone who needs to find your organization. Graphic maps, text-based directions, local hotel information, and even internal floor plans can ensure that your visitors will be able to reach you easily and efficiently.

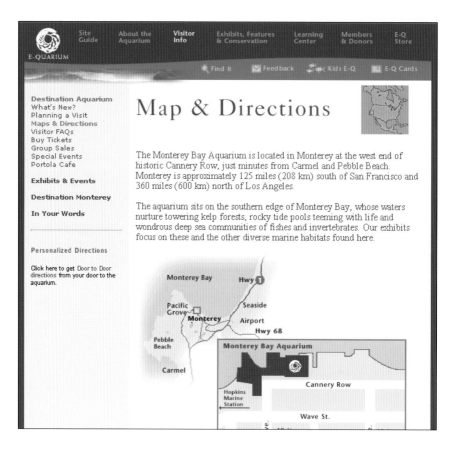

BIBLIOGRAPHIES AND APPENDIXES

The concept of "documents" in electronic environments like the Web is flexible, and the economics and logistics of digital publishing make it possible to provide information without the costs associated with printing paper documents. Making a report available to colleagues on paper usually means printing a copy for each person, so costs and practicality dictate that paper reports be concise and with limited supporting material. Bibliographies, glossaries, or appendixes that might be too bulky to load into a task force report or committee recommendations document can instead be placed in a Web site, making the information available to colleagues as needed.

FAQ PAGES

The Web and other Internet-based media have evolved a unique institution, the FAQ or "frequently asked questions" page, where the most commonly asked questions from users are listed along with answers. FAQ pages are ideal for Web sites designed to provide support and information to a working group within an institution or to a professional or trade group that maintains a central office staff. Most questions from new users have been asked and answered many times before. A well-designed FAQ page can improve users' understanding of the information and services offered and reduce demands on your support staff.

CUSTOM SERVER ERROR PAGES

Most Web users are familiar with the "404 error, file not found" screens that pop up on the screen when a Web server is unable to locate a page. The file may be missing because the author has moved or deleted it, or the reader may simply have typed or copied the URL of the page incorrectly. One mark of a really polished Web site is custom-designed and useful error and server message pages. Most standard error screens are generic, ugly, and uninformative. A well-designed error screen should be consistent with the graphic look and feel of the rest of the Web site. The page should offer some likely explanations for the error, suggest alternatives, and provide links to the local home page, site index, or search page:

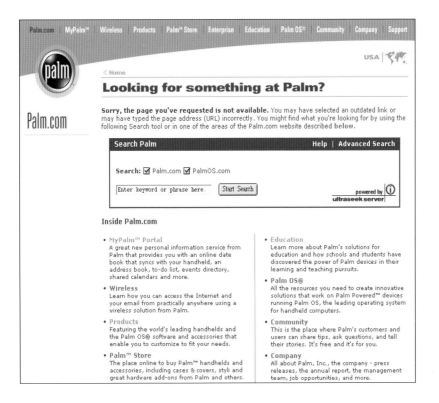

INTERNET VERSUS INTRANET DESIGN

Most Web sites are designed to be viewed by audiences inside an organization and are often not visible to the larger World Wide Web. Although these intranet sites employ the same technology as sites designed for the larger Web audience, their design and content should reflect the different motivations of intranet users.

External sites are usually aimed at capturing an audience. The overall goal is to maximize contact time, drawing readers deeper into the site and rewarding their curiosity with interesting or entertaining information. One assumption that governs Web design is that readers may have little motivation to stay and must be constantly enticed and rewarded with rich graphics or compelling information to linger within the site.

Successful intranet sites assemble useful information, organize it into logical systems, and deliver the information efficiently. You don't want intranet users lingering over their Web browsers, either in frustration at not being able to find what they are seeking or in idle "surfing." Allow employees and students to get exactly what they need quickly and then move on.

The evolution of the Web   In most institutions the use of the World Wide Web has evolved over the past few years from an informal collection of personal or group home pages into a semiorganized collection of sites listed in one or more master home pages or "front door" sites. Ironically, universities and companies that adopted the Web early are often the least organized, because each department and group has over the years evolved its own idiosyncratic approach to graphic design, user interface design, and information architecture. But the Web and institutional intranets are no longer just a playground for the local "geeks." Patchy, heterogeneous design standards and a lack of cohesive central planning can cripple any attempt to realize productivity gains through an intranet.

IBM's sites are models of a consistent, in-depth approach to Web design, making it possible for both employees and customers to navigate through a huge, complex information system with one unified visual identity and user interface:

User surveys done at Sun Microsystems in the mid-1990s by user interface expert Jakob Nielsen showed that the average Sun employee used about twelve intranet pages a day and about two new intranet subsites each week, and the numbers are surely many times higher today. Nielsen estimated that his redesign of Sun's intranet user interface would save each employee as much as five minutes a week through consistent companywide application of design and navigation interface standards. The aggregate savings in Sun employee time could amount to as much as ten million dollars a year, through improving productivity and increasing the efficiency with which employees use the company's intranet sites. Consistent, predictable interfaces are the key to a return on the enormous investment enterprises have made in their Web sites and corporate intranets.

DESIGN STANDARDS

All institutions that deploy intranets have clear economic and social motivations to develop and propagate a consistent set of design standards for the development of local Web pages and internal information sources. But obstacles to implementing an institutionwide set of standards are considerable. Groups and individuals may feel that they own the "right" to design and publish as they please, and they often have more Web expertise and experience than senior management. Groups that have used the Web for years already have a considerable investment in their designs and will be reluctant to change. University and nonprofit administrations often lack the economic resources to develop institutional standards manuals and motivate departments to adopt them. The lack of broad consensus on what constitutes proper Web design only complicates the matter.

Consider the overall effect of the National Oceanic and Atmospheric Administration's home page and a few of the major pages just below the home page:

Home page

Internal pages,
same organization

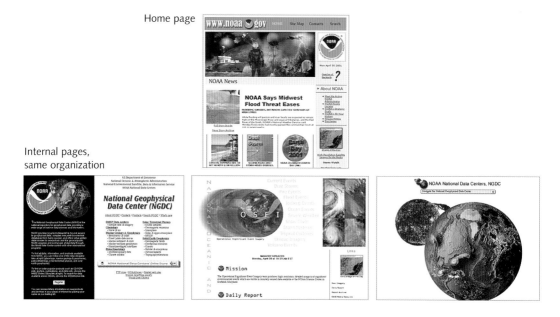

Although each individual site has its merits, in aggregate the user's experience in navigating though the various NOAA sites is cluttered, confusing, and inconsistent in visual identity and user interface. NOAA is hardly alone in this; in the rush to build Web sites most enterprises have produced crazy quilts of inconsistent designs and user interfaces and only now are realizing how painfully visible their confusion and lack of organization are to the outside world. Never judge the success of your particular site design by looking only within the bounds of your enterprise's site. Readers spend most of their time on sites other than your little slice of the Web. The only way to create a sustained and consistent sense of place and easy navigation is to establish broad consensus within the larger enterprise and create sites that look and feel like a consistent whole.

User-centered design The design and interface problems cited above will be familiar to every corporate or enterprise Webmaster and to anyone who has had to sit on a Web or intranet committee. The human and technical difficulties are all great reasons for doing nothing, but they ignore the most important element of any Web site: the user. If reasonable, consistent design standards are not adopted, the average user suffers confusion, reduced productivity, and lost opportunity to benefit from the promise of Web information sources. The advantages of consistent graphic design and user interface standards are immediately obvious in a user-centered approach to Web design and clearly transcend the parochial interests of participating departments, groups, and individuals. If the typical user of a public site or corporate intranet sees more confusion than useful information, no one will benefit.

Without clear design standards, your overall enterprise Web presence will evolve as a patchy, confusing set of pages—some well designed, some disastrous, and all mere parts of a dysfunctional system. A lack of design standards also limits Web use by imposing complex design decisions on new users who would like to develop sites; it's a daunting task to have to develop new graphic design and interface conventions instead of being able to adopt a professionally designed system of corporate intranet standards.

REFERENCES

Fleming, Jennifer. 1998. *Web navigation: Designing the user experience*. Sebastopol, Calif.: O'Reilly.

Harrower, Tim. 1998. *The newspaper designer's handbook*, 4th ed. Boston:
McGraw-Hill.

Krug, Steve. 2001. *Don't make me think! A common sense approach to Web
usability*. Indianapolis, Ind.: Que.

Nielsen, Jakob. 1995. *The alertbox: Current issues in Web usability*. http://
www.useit.com/alertbox.

———. 1999. *Designing Web usability: The practice of simplicity*. Indianapolis, Ind.: New Riders.

Rosenfeld, Louis, and Peter Morville. 1998. *Information architecture for the
World Wide Web*. Sebastopol, Calif.: O'Reilly.

Sklar, Joel. 2000. *Principles of Web design*. Cambridge, Mass.: Course Technology.

Veen, Jeffrey. 2001. *The art and science of Web design*. Indianapolis, Ind.:
New Riders.

4 **Page Design**

If you ask why something works and you push back far enough,
eventually everything seems to be based on contrast: the ability to
distinguish one thing from another. Composition, sequencing, even
legibility all rely on devices that affect the contrast between things.
—Chris Pulman, *The Education of a Graphic Designer*

WE SEEK CLARITY, order, and trustworthiness in information sources, whether traditional paper documents or Web pages. Effective page design can provide this confidence. The spatial organization of graphics and text on the Web page can engage readers with graphic impact, direct their attention, prioritize the information they see, and make their interactions with your Web site more enjoyable and efficient.

Visual logic Graphic design creates visual logic and seeks an optimal balance between visual sensation and graphic information. Without the visual impact of shape, color, and contrast, pages are graphically uninteresting and will not motivate the viewer. Dense text documents without contrast and visual relief are also harder to read, particularly on the relatively low-resolution screens of personal computers. But without the depth and complexity of text, highly graphical pages risk disappointing the user by offering a poor balance of visual sensation, text information, and interactive hypermedia links. In seeking this ideal balance, the primary design constraints are the restrictions of HTML and the bandwidth limitations on user access ranging from slow modems to high-speed connections such as Ethernet or DSL.

Visual and functional continuity in your Web site organization, graphic design, and typography are essential to convince your audience that your Web site offers them timely, accurate, and useful information. A careful, systematic approach to page design can simplify navigation, reduce user errors, and make it easier for readers to take advantage of the information and features of the site.

VISUAL HIERARCHY

The primary task of graphic design is to create a strong, consistent visual hierarchy in which important elements are emphasized and content is organized logically and predictably.

Graphic design is visual information management, using the tools of page layout, typography, and illustration to lead the reader's eye through the page. Readers first see pages as large masses of shape and color, with foreground elements contrasting against the background field. Secondarily they begin to pick out specific information, first from graphics if they are present, and only then do they start parsing the harder medium of text and begin to read individual words and phrases:

Visual scanning of page structure over time

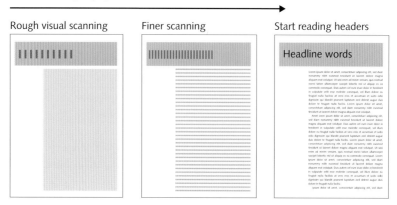

Rough visual scanning   Finer scanning   Start reading headers

Contrast is essential   The overall graphic balance and organization of the page is crucial to drawing the reader into your content. A dull page of solid text will repel the eye as a mass of undifferentiated gray, without obvious cues to the structure of your information. A page dominated by poorly designed or overly bold graphics or typography will also distract or repel users looking for substantive content. You will need to strike an appropriate balance between attracting the eye with visual contrast and providing a sense of organization:

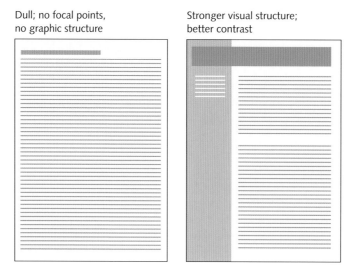

Dull; no focal points, no graphic structure   Stronger visual structure; better contrast

Visual balance and appropriateness to the intended audience are the keys to successful design decisions. The most effective designs for general Internet audiences use a careful balance of text and links with relatively small graphics. These pages load into browsers quickly, even when accessed from slow modems, yet still achieve substantial graphic impact:

When establishing a page design for your Web site, consider your overall purpose, the nature of your content, and, most important, the expectations of your readers.

CONSISTENCY

Establish a layout grid and a style for handling your text and graphics, then apply it consistently to build rhythm and unity across the pages of your site. Repetition is not boring; it gives your site a consistent graphic identity that creates and then reinforces a distinct sense of "place" and makes your site memorable. A consistent approach to layout and navigation allows readers to adapt quickly to your design and to confidently predict the location of information and navigation controls across the pages of your site.

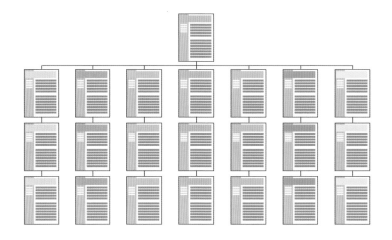

If you choose a graphic theme, use it throughout your Web site. The Bridgeman Art Library home page banner, below, sets the graphic theme for the site and introduces distinctive typography and a set of navigation buttons:

Below is a banner at the top of an interior page in the Bridgeman Art Library site. Note how the typography and the navigation theme are carried over to the interior banners. There is no confusion about whose site you are navigating through:

PAGE DIMENSIONS

Although Web pages and conventional print documents share many graphic, functional, and editorial similarities, the computer screen, not the printed page, is the primary delivery site for Web-based information, and the computer screen is very different from the printed page. Computer screens are typically smaller than most opened books or magazines. A common mistake in Web design is spreading the width of page graphics beyond the area most viewers can see on their seventeen- or nineteen-inch display screens:

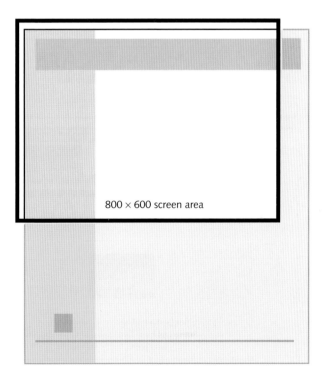

800 × 600 screen area

The "safe area" for Web page graphics is determined by two factors: the minimum screen size in common use and the width of paper used to print Web pages.

Most display screens used in academia and business are seventeen to nineteen inches (forty-three to forty-eight centimeters) in size, and most are set to display an 800 × 600-pixel screen. Web page graphics that exceed the width dimension of the most common display screens look amateurish and will inconvenience many readers by forcing them to scroll both horizontally and vertically to see the full page layout. It's bad enough to have to scroll in one (vertical) direction; having to scroll in two directions is intolerable.

Too-wide layout does not fit on 800 x 600 screen

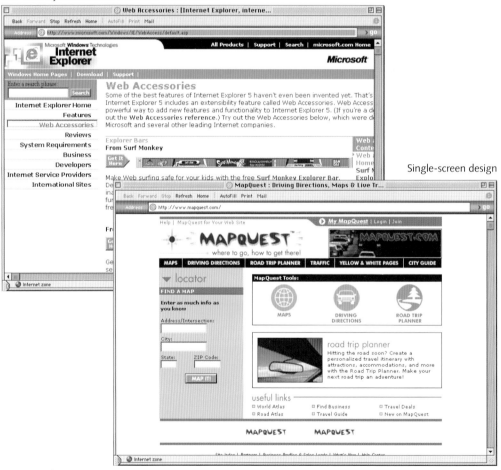

Single-screen design

Even on small computer screens it is possible to display graphics that are too wide to print well on common letter-size, legal-size, or A4 paper widths. Current browser versions attempt to resolve printing problems by providing the option to scale the page contents to fit the standard paper width. However, many users are unaware of the "fit to page" option. Another problem is that wide pages that are scaled to fit are often illegible because the type has been scaled excessively. In many Web pages, however, printing is a secondary concern. Just be aware that your readers will either lose the right margin of your layout or produce a scaled document if they print wide pages in standard vertical print layout. Pages with lots of text should *always* be designed to print properly because most readers will print those pages to read them more comfortably. If the page layout is too wide readers will lose several words from each line of text down the right margin or have to contend with small type.

The graphic safe area dimensions for printing layouts and for page layouts designed to use the maximum width of 800 × 600 screens are shown below:

Graphic "safe area" dimensions for layouts designed to print well:
Maximum width = 560 pixels
Maximum height = 410 pixels (visible without scrolling)

Graphic "safe area" dimensions for layouts designed for 800 × 600 screens:
Maximum width = 760 pixels
Maximum height = 410 pixels (visible without scrolling)

Graphic safe areas, 800 × 600 screens
Dimensions account for both Netscape Navigator and Internet Explorer, in both Windows/NT and Macintosh versions. Note that if you choose to maximize the width of your page layout, you may lose about two centimeters off the right edge of the page when it is printed

PAGE LENGTH

Determining the proper length for any Web page requires balancing four factors:

1 The relation between page and screen size
2 The content of your documents
3 Whether the reader is expected to browse the content online or to print or download the documents for later reading
4 The bandwidth available to your audience

Researchers have noted the disorientation that results from scrolling on computer screens. The reader's loss of context is particularly troublesome when such basic navigational elements as document titles, site identifiers, and links to other site pages disappear off-screen while scrolling. This disorientation effect argues for the creation of navigational Web pages (especially home pages and menus) that contain no more than one or two screens' worth of information and that feature local navigational links at the beginning and end of the page layout. Long Web pages require the user to remember too much information that scrolls off the screen; users easily lose their sense of context when the navigational buttons or major links are not visible:

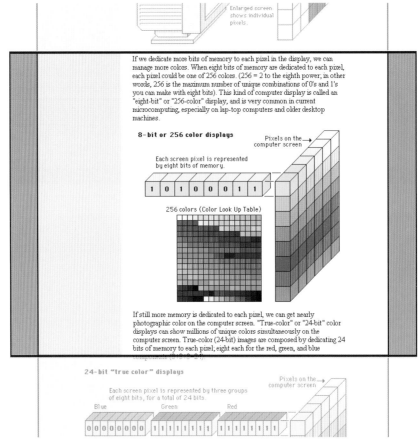

Scrolling In long Web pages the user must depend on the vertical scroll bar slider (the sliding box within the scroll bar) to navigate. In some graphic interfaces the scroll bar slider is fixed in size and provides little indication of the document length relative to what's visible on the screen, so the reader gets no visual cue to page length. In very long Web pages small movements of the scroll bar can completely change the visual contents of the screen, leaving the reader no familiar landmarks to orient by. This gives the user no choice but to crawl downward with the scroll bar arrows or risk missing sections of the page.

Long Web pages do have their advantages, however. They are often easier for creators to organize and for users to download. Web site managers don't have to maintain as many links and pages with longer documents, and users don't need to download multiple files to collect information on a topic. Long pages are particularly useful for providing information that you don't expect users to read online (realistically, that means any document longer than two printed pages). You can make long pages friendlier by positioning "jump to top buttons" at regular intervals down the page. That way the user will never have to scroll far to find a navigation button that quickly brings him or her back to the top of the page.

▲   Return to main Community Service page

Health

AIDS

- ○ Adolescent Clinic: AIDS Education in High Schools (AIDS Care Program and Yale-New Haven Hospital)
- ○ Family Support Program for HIV-infected children (Pediatrics)
- ○ Mobile Van - accompanies the city's Needle Exchange Program (School of Medicine)
- ○ Students Teaching AIDS to Students (STATS) (Committee Overseeing Volunteer Services)
- ○ Volunteer Nurse Program at the AIDS Project (School of Nursing)

▲   Return to main Community Service page

Asthma

- ○ Allergy and Asthma and Clinical Immunology Adult Clinic (Internal Medicine) 785-4629
- ○ Allergy and Sinus Disease Clinic (Internal Medicine/ENT) 737-4043
- ○ Asthma and Asthma Medication Use in Pregnancy (Perinatal Epidemiology Unit)
- ○ Childhood Asthma Study (Perinatal Epidemiology Unit)

▲   Return to main Community Service page

Cancer

- ○ Breast and Cervical Cancer Screening Program (Yale-New

All Web pages longer than two vertical screens should have a jump button at the foot of the page:

Jump to top of page

If a Web page is too long, however, or contains too many large graphics, the page can take too long for users with slow connections to download. Very large Web pages with many graphics may also overwhelm the RAM (random access memory) limitations of the user's Web browser, causing the browser to crash or causing the page to display and print improperly.

CONTENT AND PAGE LENGTH

It makes sense to keep closely related information within the confines of a single Web page, particularly when you expect the user to print or save the text. Keeping the content in one place makes printing or saving easier. But more than four screens' worth of information forces the user to scroll so much that the utility of the online version of the page begins to deteriorate. Long pages often fail to take advantage of the linkages available in the Web medium.

If you wish to provide both a good online interface for a long document and easy printing or saving of its content:

- Divide the document into chunks of no more than one to two printed pages' worth of information, including inlined graphics or figures. Use the power of hypertext links to take advantage of the Web medium.
- Provide a link to a separate file that contains the full-length text combined as one page designed so the reader can print or save all the related information in one step. Don't forget to include the URL of the online version within the text of that page so users can find updates and correctly cite the source.

In general, you should favor shorter Web pages for:
- Home pages and menu or navigation pages elsewhere in your site
- Documents to be browsed and read online
- Pages with very large graphics

In general, longer documents are:
- Easier to maintain (content is in one piece, not in linked chunks)
- More like the structure of their paper counterparts (not chopped up)
- Easier for users to download and print

DESIGN GRIDS FOR WEB PAGES

Consistency and predictability are essential attributes of any well-designed information system. The design grids that underlie most well-designed paper publications are equally necessary in designing electronic documents and online publications, where the spatial relations among on-screen elements are constantly shifting in response to the user's input and system activity.

Grids bring order to the page   Current implementations of HyperText Markup Language do not allow the easy flexibility or control that graphic designers routinely expect from page layout software or multimedia authoring tools. Yet HTML can be used to create complex and highly functional information systems if it is used thoughtfully. When used inappropriately or inconsistently, the typographic controls and inlined graphics of Web pages can create a confusing visual jumble, without apparent hierarchy of importance. Haphazardly mixed graphics and text decrease usability and legibility, just as they do in paper pages. A balanced and consistently implemented design scheme will increase readers' confidence in your site.

Poor page layout, no visual hierarchy   Better layout, balanced

No one design grid system is appropriate for all Web pages. Your first step is to establish a basic layout grid. With this graphic "backbone" you can determine how the major blocks of type and illustrations will regularly occur in your pages and set the placement and style guidelines for major screen titles, subtitles, and navigation links or buttons. To start, gather representative examples of your text, along with some graphics, scans, or other illustrative material, and experiment with various arrangements of the elements on the page. In larger projects it isn't possible to exactly predict how every combination of text and graphics will interact on the screen, but examine your Web layout "sketches" against both your most complex and your least complex pages.

Your goal is to establish a consistent, logical screen layout, one that allows you to "plug in" text and graphics without having to stop and rethink your basic design approach on each new page. Without a firm underlying design grid, your project's page layout will be driven by the problems of the moment, and the overall design of your Web site will seem patchy and confusing.

Vertical stratification in Web pages   A Web page can be almost any length, but you've only got about forty-five square inches "above the fold"—at the top of your page—to capture the average reader, because that is all he or she will see as the page loads. One crucial difference between Web page design and print page design is that when readers turn a book or magazine page they see not only the whole next page but the whole two-page spread, all at the same time. In print design, therefore, the two-page spread is the fundamental graphic design unit.

Print design can achieve a design unity and density of information that Web page design cannot emulate. Regardless of how large the display screen is, the reader still sees one page at a time, and even a twenty-one-inch screen will display only as much information as is found in a small magazine spread:

Book pages

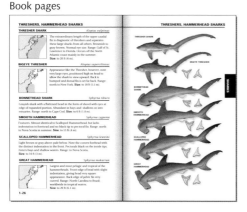

Web page on a seventeen-inch monitor (1024 × 768 pixels)

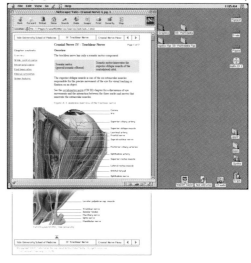

Book spreads are seen as units of two pages; Web pages are always single units, regardless of monitor size

Design for screens of information   Most Web page designs can be divided vertically into zones with different functions and varying levels of graphics and text complexity. As vertical scrolling progressively reveals the page, new content appears and the upper content disappears. A new graphic context is established each time the reader scrolls down the page. Web page layouts should thus be judged not by viewing the whole page as a unit but by dividing the page into visual and functional zones and judging the suitability of each screen of information. Notice the vertical structure of the home page reproduced below. The top screen of information is much denser with links because it is the only area that is sure to be visible to all users:

First screen
• Highest priority items
• Most graphics
• Highest density of links

(Density: 25 links)

"Above the fold"

"Below the fold"

Second screen
• Lower priority items
• Less graphic
• Density of links less critical

PAGE HEADERS AND FOOTERS

Many Web authors surrender to the giddy thrills of large home page graphics, forgetting that a Web page is not just a visual experience—it has to function efficiently to retain its appeal to the user. Remember that the page builds its graphic impact only gradually as it is downloaded to the user. The best measure of the efficiency of a page design is the number of options available for readers within the top four inches of the page. A big, bold graphic may tease casual Web surfers, but if it takes the average reader thirty seconds to download the top of your page, and there are few links to be seen until he or she scrolls down the page (causing even longer delays), then you may lose a big part of your audience before you offer them links to the rest of your site.

PAGE HEADERS: SITE IDENTITY

Careful graphic design will give your Web site a unique visual identity. A "signature" graphic and page layout allows the reader to grasp immediately the purpose of the document and its relation to other pages. Graphics used within headers can also signal the relatedness of a series of Web pages. Unlike designers of print documents, designers of Web systems can never be sure what other pages the reader has seen before linking to the current page. Sun Microsystems's many Web pages and subsites all include a signature header graphic that includes basic navigation links:

Even if you choose not to use graphics on your pages, the header area of every Web page should contain a prominent title at or near its top. Graphics placed above the title line should not be so large that they force the title and introductory text off the page on standard office-size display screens. In a related series of documents there may also be subtitles, section titles, or other text elements that convey the relation of the displayed document to others in the series. To be effective, these title elements must be standardized across all the pages in your site.

PAGE FOOTERS: PROVENANCE

Every Web page should contain basic data about the origin and age of the page, but this repetitive and prosaic information does not need to be placed at the top of the page. Remember, too, that by the time readers have scrolled to the bottom of your Web page the navigation links you might have provided at the top may no longer be visible. Well-designed page footers offer the user a set of links to other pages in addition to essential data about the site.

The pages in the IBM Web site all carry a distinctive footer graphic with a consistent visual and functional identity:

PAGE LAYOUT

Laying out Web pages involves a bit of wizardry. HTML was designed by engineers and scientists who never envisioned it as a page layout tool. Their aim was to provide a way to describe structural information about a document, not a tool to determine a document's appearance. Once the real world started to work on the Web, graphic designers began adapting the primitive tools of HTML to produce documents that looked more like their print counterparts. The point was not to produce "jazzier" or "prettier" pages. The layout conventions of print documents have evolved over hundreds of years for concrete and practical reasons, and they offer many functional advantages over the simplistic, single-column page layout envisioned by the original designers of the World Wide Web.

Summary of Section 508 Standards

- General
- Technical Standards
  - Software applications and operating systems
  - Web-based intranet and internet information and systems
  - Telecommunication products
  - Video and multimedia products
  - Self contained, closed products
  - Desktop and portable computers
- Functional Performance Criteria
- Information, Documentation, and Support

General (Subpart A)
The standards define the types of technology covered and set forth provisions that establish a minimum level of accessibility. The application section (1194.2) outlines the scope and coverage of the standards. The standards cover the full range of electronic and information technologies in the Federal sector, including those used for communication, duplication, computing, storage, presentation, control, transport and production. This includes computers, software, networks, peripherals and other types of electronic office equipment. The standards define *electronic and information technology*, in part, as "any equipment or interconnected system or subsystem of equipment, that is used in the creation, conversion, or duplication of data or information."

Subpart A also explains what is exempt (1194.3), defines terms (1194.4), and generally recognizes alternatives to what is required that provide equal or greater access (1194.5). Consistent with the law, the standards exempt systems used for military command, weaponry, intelligence, and cryptologic activities (but not routine business and administrative systems used for other defense-related purposes or by defense agencies or personnel). The standards also exempt "back office" equipment used only by service personnel for maintenance, repair, or similar purposes.

The standards cover technology procured by Federal agencies under contract with a private entity, but apply only to those products directly relevant to the contract and its deliverables. An exception clarifies that the standards do not apply to technology that is incidental to a Federal contract. Thus, those products that are not specified as part of a contract with a Federal agency would not have to comply with the standards. For example, a firm that produces a report for a Federal agency under a contract would not have to procure accessible computers and word processing software even if they were used exclusively for the contract; however, compliance would be required if such products were to become the property of the Federal agency as contract deliverables or if the Federal agency purchased the products to be used by the contractor as part of the project. If a Federal agency contracts with a firm to develop its web site the standards would apply to the new web site for the agency but not to the firm's own web site.

Flexible design   The Web is a flexible medium designed to accommodate different types of users and a variety of display devices. Unlike a printed document, which is "fixed" in its medium, the look of a Web page depends on such elements as the display size, resolution, and color settings, the height and width of the browser window, software preferences such as link and background color settings, and available fonts. Indeed, there is no way to have complete control over the design of a Web page. The best approach, then, is to embrace the medium and design flexible pages that are legible and accessible to all users.

Layout with Style Sheets   One of the visual properties that Cascading Style Sheets are meant to describe is how elements are positioned on the page. Style sheet positioning allows designers to set margins, to position text and images on the page relative to one another, to hide and show elements, and to stack elements so they overlay one another. In theory, style sheet positioning should provide all the design control needed to lay out visually appealing and legible Web pages. In practice, however, browser inconsistencies have rendered style sheet positioning useless, at least for the time being. Though the w3c specifications for style sheet positioning contain most of the tools needed for good design, Microsoft and Netscape have done a particularly poor job of implementing them, so that properties such as borders and margins display quite differently from browser to browser. If you are creating a site for a diverse audience you should steer clear of style sheet positioning for now and design your pages using layout tables as described below. If standards compliance is a priority, use style sheet positioning for page layout, but keep your layouts simple and be ready to accept variability across browsers and platforms.

LAYOUT TABLES

If you simply place a chunk of text on a Web page, the dimensions of the viewer's browser window will determine the line length. When the user resizes his or her window, the text reflows to fill the new space. Although this adaptable "feature" of Web documents is central to the premise of the Web, it can hinder the user's experience with the content. All the issues of legibility, readability, and style that we discuss in this manual rely on the Web designer's ability to position words, images, and screen elements on the "page" with some precision. Without some adherence to established typographic conventions you may confuse and ultimately lose your readers.

Because of the limitations of HTML and the inconsistencies of css, the only reliable layout tools for site designers at this time are HTML tables.

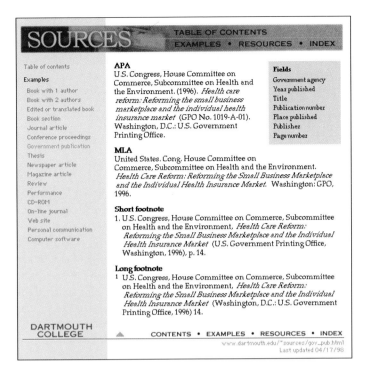

Line length   The ideal line length for text layout is based on the physiology of the human eye. The area of the retina that is used for tasks requiring high visual acuity is called the macula. The macula is small, typically less than 15 percent of the area of the retina. At normal reading distances the arc of the visual field covered by the macula is only a few inches wide—about the width of a well-designed column of text, or about twelve words per line. Research shows that reading slows and retention rates fall as line lengths begin to exceed the ideal width, because the reader then needs to use the muscles of the eye or neck to track from the end of one line to the beginning of the next line. If the eye must traverse great distances on a page, the reader is easily lost and must hunt for the beginning of the next line. Quantitative studies show that moderate line lengths significantly increase the legibility of text. Use tables to limit the line length, ideally to ten to twelve words per line.

Margins   Margins define the reading area of your page by separating the main text from nontext elements, such as interface elements and other unrelated graphics. Margins also provide contrast and visual interest. Use table cells to establish margins, and use them consistently throughout your site to provide unity.

Columns   One common use of tables that increases both legibility and functionality of page layouts is a multicolumn layout, with the page divided into columns of main text, site navigation, and perhaps a third column with page-level navigation, pull-quotes, and links to related sites. Multiple columns provide a flexible space for variations in page layout and narrow the text column to a comfortable line length.

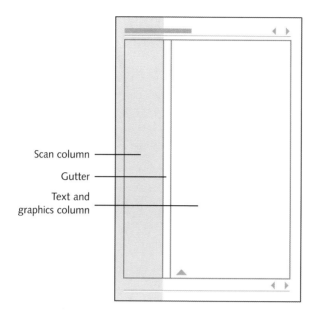

Scan column

Gutter

Text and graphics column

Gutters   In print the space between columns is called a gutter. Gutters keep columns from running into one another:

Columns without gutter

You can use tables to create gutters in three ways: (1) by adding a cell to your table that functions as the gutter, (2) by using the CELLPADDING attribute of the TABLE tag (the space between the cell contents and the cell), and (3) by using the CELLSPACING attribute of the TABLE tag (the space surrounding the cell):

Table with cell gutter

Table with CELLPADDING

Table with CELLSPACING

Borders   When we talk about tables we are not speaking of the beveled beauties that HTML offers to present tabular content. We are using tables to get around the limitations of HTML, and we are using them in ways for which they were not intended. These are invisible tables whose sole purpose is to give us control over page elements, so be sure to set BORDER="0" in your TABLE tag. And if you do use tables to present tabular information, use spacing, alignment, and indents, not borders, to delimit tabular information.

ChemLab

| Info | Techniques | Chem 3/5 | Chem 6 |

The Chemistry 3/5 Laboratory

Week 6: Acids, bases, and buffers, cont.

Introduction & goals

Chemistry & background

Key questions

Prelab problems

Safety

Procedures

In your write-up

Back to Experiments

ChemLab Home

Possible Unknown Acids, Bases, and Buffers

This Table contains the possible acids and conjugate acids of possible bases. Buffers could be composed of any tabulated acid and its conjugate base.

Table 1: Weak Acids, Ka, and pKa values

Acid	HA	A^-	K_a	pKa
Acetic	CH_3COOH	CH_3COO^-	1.76×10^{-5}	4.75
Ammonium Ion	NH_4^+	NH_3	5.6×10^{-10}	9.25
Benzoic	C_6H_5COOH	$C_6H_5COO^-$	6.46×10^{-5}	4.19
Carbonic	H_2CO_3	HCO_3^-	4.3×10^{-7}	6.37
	HCO_3^-	CO_3^{2-}	4.8×10^{-11}	10.32
Chloroacetic	$CH_2ClCOOH$	CH_2ClCOO^-	1.4×10^{-3}	2.85
Formic	$HCOOH$	$HCOO^-$	1.77×10^{-4}	3.75
Oxalic	$H_2C_2O_4$	$HC_2O_4^-$	5.9×10^{-2}	1.23
	$HC_2O_4^-$	$C_2O_4^{2-}$	6.4×10^{-5}	4.19
Phosphoric	H_3PO_4	$H_2PO_4^-$	7.52×10^{-3}	2.12
	$H_2PO_4^-$	HPO_4^{-2}	6.23×10^{-8}	7.21
	HPO_4^{2-}	PO_4^{3-}	2.2×10^{-13}	12.67

ChemLab   ▲

The behavior of an HTML table depends largely on how its cells are defined. One "feature" of tables is that they try to be accommodating; they expand and collapse to accommodate their contents and to fit the dimensions of the viewer's browser window. In their most basic form, tables are not much more precise than plain text.

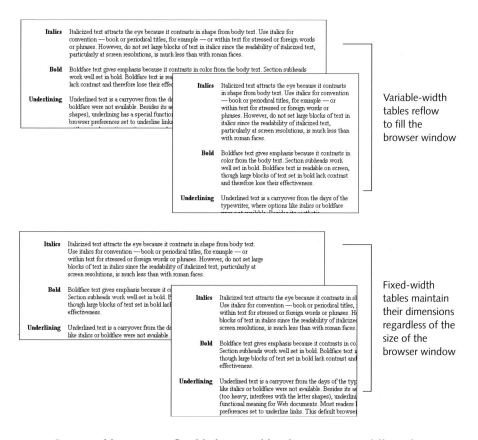

Variable-width tables reflow to fill the browser window

Fixed-width tables maintain their dimensions regardless of the size of the browser window

It is possible to create flexible layout tables that resize gracefully without sacrificing the integrity of your design, but if you are turning to layout tables for precision you will need to use fixed-width layout tables.

Use fixed-width tables for precise layouts Putting content into a fixed-width table means that your page layout will be stable whatever the size of the user's screen or browser window. Designing in a stable environment means that you can fix the position of elements on the page and control typographic features such as line length and spacing. A downside of a controlled layout is that on large display screens a major portion of screen real estate goes unused. You can avoid the "wasteland" effect of a fixed layout by centering the table in the browser window or by designing a background graphic to fill the empty areas of the screen.

Layout centered within the browser window

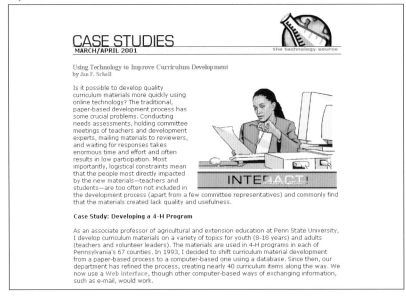

Flush-left layout with background pattern on the right for balance

In a fixed-width table you must define cell widths with absolute values. This will keep the tables from expanding to fill the window. Then, to keep tables from collapsing when the browser window is too small to accommodate their dimensions, include an invisible image equal to the width of the cell in each table cell. These two techniques will force table cells to maintain their dimensions regardless of the size of the browser window.

Main table width 550 pixels

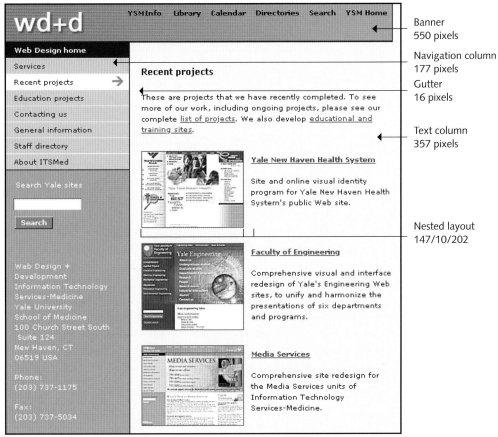

Banner
550 pixels

Navigation column
177 pixels

Gutter
16 pixels

Text column
357 pixels

Nested layout
147/10/202

Use flexible tables for layouts that adapt A popular viewpoint is that designers should embrace the nature of Web documents and create flexible layouts that adapt to different viewing conditions. To do this, you need to be willing to abandon control of aspects of your page design, notably line length. Flexible design is in many ways more challenging than fixed design because it requires a deep understanding of HTML and its implementation across platforms and browsers. It also requires that you think "outside the box" of your own configuration and come up with graphics and layouts that will still "work" under varying viewing conditions.

Tables are inherently flexible, so one approach to flexible design is to let table cells size themselves according to their contents and the size of the browser window. Another approach is to specify cell widths using percentage values; for example, set the left scan column width to 40 percent and the main text column width to 60 percent. That way the columns will resize when the window size is changed, but they will always maintain their relative proportions regardless of the size of the browser window. You can also use a combination of fixed and unspecified table cell widths to create a flexible layout. Using this technique you specify in pixels the width of the columns that require absolute positioning—for example, a navigation column or gutter—and leave the remaining column, such as the text column, unspecified so that it adapts to fill the screen.

Main table width 85% of browser window

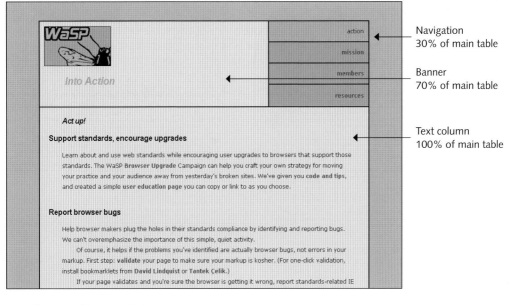

Navigation
30% of main table

Banner
70% of main table

Text column
100% of main table

Overall table width unspecified

Page links
172 pixels

Navigation column
148 pixels

Text column
width unspecified

Spacing and alignment   Tables can be used to combine different text alignments on the page. In this example the text in the left column is right justified, and the text in the right is left justified.

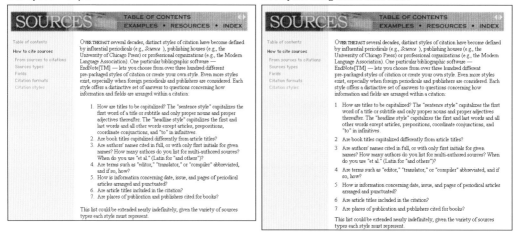

Right-aligned headers   Left-justified body text   Same page table with BORDER="0"

Tables can also be used to format such elements as bulleted lists or indents. For example, even with the aid of style sheets, the BLOCKQUOTE or list elements of HTML may produce clumsy-looking results, with overly indented text and excessive white space. You can use invisible tables to control more precisely how these typographic devices render on the page.

List layout with plain HTML

List layout using an invisible table

Colored backgrounds   You can use tables to color areas of your pages by placing the BGCOLOR attribute in your table tag and assigning it a color. You can color an entire table, a table row, or an individual table cell. Table coloring is an easy, low-bandwidth approach to adding visual identity and structure to a page without relying on graphics.

Working with images   Tables give the designer much greater flexibility in positioning images on a page than simple inline image placement. You can use tables to create complex layouts that combine text and images or multimedia materials. The example below is shown with borders both on and off to depict the underlying table used to establish the layout:

Standard two-column page table

Embedded
table for
indented
menu

Embedded
right-justified
table for image
and caption

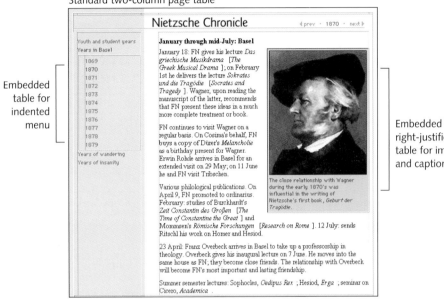

Same page table with BORDER="0"

Something fancy you can do with tables is to take a composite image, split it in pieces, and then recombine it in the cells of a table. This technique is useful for creating wraparound effects, image captions, or rollovers. The following example is depicted with borders on and off to show how the table is formatted:

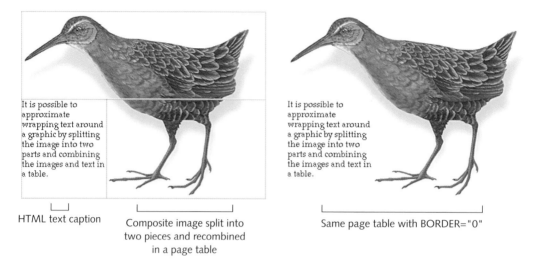

It is possible to approximate wrapping text around a graphic by splitting the image into two parts and combining the images and text in a table.

It is possible to approximate wrapping text around a graphic by splitting the image into two parts and combining the images and text in a table.

HTML text caption   Composite image split into
                         two pieces and recombined
                         in a page table

Same page table with BORDER="0"

Watch out for hard returns in your HTML code when using tables to join an image. A hard return before a closing table data tag (</TD>) will add space between the table cells. You will also need to set the CELLPADDING, CELLSPACING, and BORDER parameters of the TABLE tag to zero in order for the image to join correctly. Finally, be sure to include an invisible image to keep the cells in your tables from collapsing (see the section on fixed-width tables, above).

FRAMES

Frames are *meta*-documents that call and display multiple HTML documents in a single browser window. A frame document contains no BODY HTML tags, just the parameters for the frames and the URLs of the HTML documents designated to fill them. Frames-based pages do not function as an integrated unit, which is both good and bad. Frames are useful for certain content and greatly facilitate site maintenance. They provide a good way to maintain narrative and design consistency in your site; you can split the browser screen between site navigation and the material you wish to bring up with a link.

But frames also impose interface and design limitations. Frames can easily confuse readers who wish to print material on a page or bookmark a page for later reference or navigate using the browser's "Forward" and "Back" buttons. And screen space becomes an issue with frames; if you use frames to divide the browser screen, you will force many readers to scroll both horizontally and vertically to see the full contents of each frame. The current consensus among Web design and usability experts is that frames should be used only in the rare instances when their limited advantages clearly outweigh the many problems they can cause.

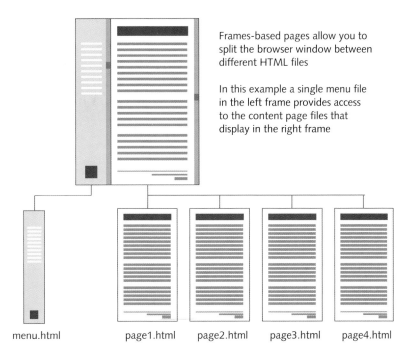

Frames-based pages allow you to split the browser window between different HTML files

In this example a single menu file in the left frame provides access to the content page files that display in the right frame

menu.html   page1.html   page2.html   page3.html   page4.html

Flexibility   Frames are useful in a site whose contents are expected to change frequently. Because a frames-based site can be designed to have a single file for navigation, if you add or remove pages from the site you will have to modify only that one file. Our online Web Style Guide, for example, requires that a number of files be changed if we add or delete a page because each page in the site has its own navigation. If we had used frames in our design, we would have had a single file for the section menu, and when we needed to add a page, only that file would have had to be changed to reflect the addition. As it is, when we add a page to a section we must edit each file in that section to add the new link.

Functionality   Frames can give a targeted area of your site a functional coherence. Say your site contains a collection of poems by Emily Dickinson. You could create a virtual "reading room" for her poetry using frames, with the leftmost frame providing the navigation links and the main frame at the right displaying the poems. Because most visitors linger in this area and would use the links you provide for navigation, the quirky navigation of the "Back" button would not be too intrusive.

You can also use frames to provide additional interactivity to your page. Frames allow you to put a page up on the user's screen and change its contents without rewriting the screen. The frames can interact; clicking a link in one frame can change the contents of the other. For example, a text with annotations in one frame can be linked to a footer frame, so that clicking on the text reference fills the footer frame with the corresponding note:

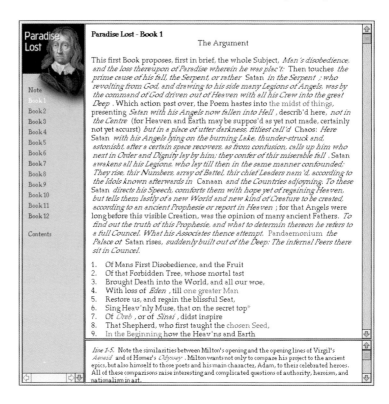

Aesthetics   Many page designers have avoided frames because of their prescribed borders and limited flexibility. Current versions of browser software, however, allow many more frame parameters to be defined. In fact, frame borders can now be set to zero. This allows you to design using the functionality of frames without requiring them to be visual and perhaps inharmonious elements on your page.

Frame titles   The visual relationship between the content in frames is usually obvious for users who can see: for example, navigation links in the left frame, content in the right. Without the benefit of visual cues, however, blind users will have difficulty orienting themselves in a frames-based layout. As discussed above, there are many reasons to avoid a frames-based layout, but if you must use frames, be sure to include titles for FRAMESET tags and a NOFRAMES alternative to navigating your site.

```
<FRAMESET COLS="20%, 80%" TITLE="Web Style Guide">
<FRAME SRC="nav.html" TITLE="Navigation">
<FRAME SRC="chapter1.html" TITLE="Chapter 1: Process">
```

```
< NOFRAMES><A HREF="content.html" TITLE="Table of Content">Web Style
    Guide Table of Contents</A>
</NOFRAMES>
</FRAMESET>
```

GENERAL DESIGN CONSIDERATIONS

Understand the medium　　Readers experience Web pages in two ways: as a direct medium where pages are read online and as a delivery medium to access information that is downloaded into text files or printed onto paper. Your expectations about how readers will typically use your site should govern your page design decisions. Documents to be read online should be concise, with the amount of graphics carefully "tuned" to the bandwidth available to your mainstream audience. Documents that will most likely be printed and read offline should appear on one page, and the page width should be narrow enough to print easily on standard paper sizes.

Include fixed page elements　　Each page should contain a title, an author, an institutional affiliation, a revision date, copyright information, and a link to the "home page" of your site. Web pages are often printed or saved to disk, and without this information there is no easy way to determine where the document originated. Think of each page in your site as a newspaper clipping, and make sure that the information required to determine its provenance is included.

Don't impose style　　Don't set out to develop a "style" for your site, and be careful about simply importing the graphic elements of another Web site or print publication to "decorate" your pages. The graphic and editorial style of your Web site should evolve as a natural consequence of consistent and appropriate handling of your content and page layout.

Maximize prime real estate　　In page layout the top of the page is always the most dominant location, but on Web pages the upper page is especially important, because the top four inches of the page are all that is visible on the typical display screen. Use this space efficiently and effectively.

Use subtle colors　　Subtle pastel shades of colors typically found in nature make the best choices for background or minor elements. Avoid bold, highly saturated primary colors except in regions of maximum emphasis, and even there use them cautiously.

Beware of graphic embellishments　　Horizontal rules, graphic bullets, icons, and other visual markers have their occasional uses, but apply each sparingly (if at all) to avoid a patchy and confusing layout. The same consideration applies to the larger sizes of type on Web pages. One reason professional graphic designers are so impatient with plain HTML is that the H1 and H2 header tags display in grotesquely large type on most Web browsers. The tools of graphic emphasis are powerful and should be used only in small doses for maximum effect. Overuse of graphic emphasis leads to a "clown's pants" effect in which everything is garish and nothing is emphasized.

CROSS-PLATFORM ISSUES

Browser variations   Every Web browser interprets HTML and CSS tags a little differently. Tables, forms, and graphic positioning and alignment tags will all work a bit differently in each brand or operating system version of Web browser. These subtleties normally pass unnoticed, but in very precise or complex Web page layouts they can lead to nasty surprises. Never trust the implementation of HTML, CSS, JavaScript, Java, or any plug-in architecture until you have seen your Web pages displayed and working reliably in each brand of browser. If significant numbers of your readers are using the Macintosh, Linux, or UNIX operating systems, you should also test your more complex pages and programming functionality in those operating systems. Unfortunately, platform-specific bugs remain common in the major Web browsers.

ACCESSIBILITY

Many accessibility issues have to do with presenting certain types of content, and these are covered in the chapters on typography, graphics, and multimedia. But you can take measures with your page design to improve access for users with physical disabilities, particularly those who use assistive technologies to access Web pages. There are also basic decisions you'll need to make about your design approach: whether to adopt a no-holds-barred stance and push the boundaries of Web design or create simple, clear designs that will accommodate all users.

Layout tables that make sense   The biggest page-design barrier for disabled users is the use of layout tables. In particular, layout tables can make things unpleasant for blind users. Many blind users rely on software that reads Web pages aloud or outputs information to a speech synthesizer or braille display. Current software looks at the HTML code of the pages and reads tables in a cell-by-cell, or *linearized*, fashion. This means that each cell of the table becomes a line or paragraph of text that is read in sequence (imagine releasing all content from table cells and displaying it down a single-column page). A complex layout containing multiple nested tables will produce a sort of aural cubism, with unrelated bits of information appearing from nowhere and disrupting the natural flow of the content. Worse still is the case with older screen readers, which look not at source code but instead at the rendered page. This software starts at the top left of the page and reads line by line, producing a garbled stream of gibberish for the multicolumn layouts that are so common on the Web.

Some screen reader software linearizes tables, which can wreak havoc on a multi-column layout

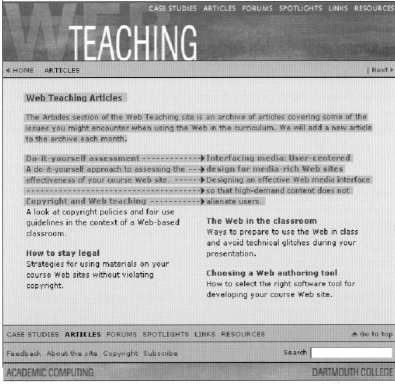

The best solution is to use CSS instead of layout tables to create columns and to control spacing, but as discussed above, browser support remains too patchy and inconsistent for style sheet positioning to be a real option (see *Layout with Style Sheets,* above). Until CSS support improves, keep your use of layout tables simple and clean. Each time you add another nested table, first consider whether it is essential to your design and if the function could be handled some other way. The simpler the table, the better sense it will make when linearized.

Alternatives   Attention to accessibility needn't squelch the creative and experimental nature of Web design. There *is* room on the Web for designs based on complex tables, large graphics, and technologies such as Flash, but these pages need to come with an equivalent, accessible version. If there is simply no way to design your primary pages for access, provide a link to an alternative page containing the same or equivalent content in a more accessible format.

If you use graphics for navigation, be sure to include redundant text links so that those users who cannot see your graphics have an alternate method for navigating your site. Also be sure to include the ALT attribute for all graphics and imagemaps (see Chapter 7, *ALT-text*).

Clarity and consistency   All users benefit from clear and consistent Web site design, but for some users it is critical. With a lack of spatial cues and with radically different approaches to navigation that must be relearned at every site, it is far too easy to get disoriented or lost on the Web. For people with cognitive disabilities such as memory or learning disabilities, this difficulty is magnified manyfold. In the long run, there is really no place on the Web for a clever, quirky, or highfalutin design approach. Stick with a simple language and navigation applied consistently throughout your site, and everyone will benefit.

REFERENCES

Beach, M., and E. Floyd. 1998. *Newsletter sourcebook*, 2d ed. Cincinnati, Ohio: Writer's Digest.

Brewer, Judy, ed. 2001. *How people with disabilities use the Web.* http://www.w3c.org/WAI/EO/Drafts/PWD-Use-Web (31 March 2001).

Bringhurst, Robert. 1996. *The elements of typographic style*, 2d ed. Vancouver, B.C.: Hartley and Marks.

Chisholm, Wendy, Gregg Vanderheiden, and Ian Jacobs, eds. 1999. *Web content accessibility guidelines 1.0.* http://www.w3c.org/TR/WAI-WEBCONTENT/wai-pageauth.html (17 January 2001).

Harrower, Tim. 1998. *The newspaper designer's handbook*, 4th ed. Boston: McGraw-Hill.

Hurlburt, Allen. 1978. *The grid: A modular system for the design and production of newspapers, magazines, and books.* New York: Van Nostrand Reinhold.

Lie, Håkon Wium, and Bert Bos. 1999. *Cascading Style Sheets: Designing for the Web*, 2d ed. Reading, Mass.: Addison-Wesley.

Meyer, Eric A. 2000. *Cascading Style Sheets: The definitive guide.* Sebastopol, Calif.: O'Reilly.

Müller-Brockmann, Josef. 1996. *Grid systems in graphic design*, 4th ed. Basel: Verlag Niggli.

Niederst, Jennifer. 1999. *Web design in a nutshell: A desktop quick reference.* Sebastopol, Calif.: O'Reilly.

Pulman, Chris. 1998. Some things change . . . . In *The education of a graphic designer*, ed. Steven Heller. New York: Allworth.

Wilson, Adrian. 1967. *The design of books.* Salt Lake City, Utah: Peregrine Books.

5   Typography

Typography exists to honor content.
—Robert Bringhurst, *The Elements of Typographic Style*

TYPOGRAPHY is the balance and interplay of letterforms on the page, a verbal and visual equation that helps the reader understand the form and absorb the substance of the page content. Typography plays a dual role as both verbal and visual communication. As readers scan a page they are subconsciously aware of both functions: first they survey the overall graphic patterns of the page, then they parse the language, or read. Good typography establishes a visual hierarchy for rendering prose on the page by providing visual punctuation and graphic accents that help readers understand relations between prose and pictures, headlines and subordinate blocks of text.

CHARACTERISTICS OF TYPE ON THE WEB

Although the basic rules of typography are much the same for both Web pages and conventional print documents, type on-screen and type printed on paper are different in crucial ways. The computer screen renders typefaces at a much lower resolution than is found in books, magazines, and even pages output from inexpensive printers. Most magazine and book typography is rendered at 1200 dots per inch (dpi) or greater, whereas computer screens rarely show more than about 85 dpi. Also, the useable area of typical computer screens is smaller than most magazine and book pages, limiting the information you can deliver on a Web page without scrolling.

But perhaps the most distinctive characteristic of Web typography is its variability. Web pages are built on the fly each time they are loaded into a Web browser. Each line of text, each headline, each unique font and type style is re-created by a complex interaction of the Web browser, the Web server, and the operating system of the reader's computer. The process is fraught with possibilities for the unexpected: a missing font, an out-of-date browser, or a peculiar set of font preferences designated by the reader. You should regard your Web page layouts and typography as *suggestions* of how your pages should be rendered—you'll never know exactly how they will look on the reader's screen.

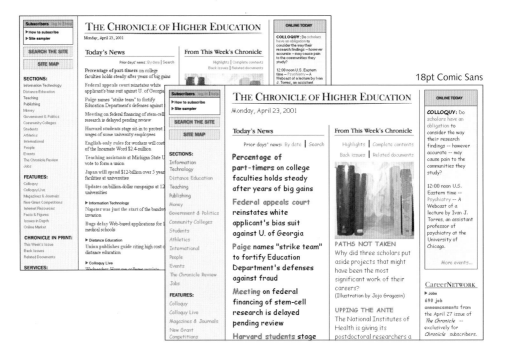

18pt Comic Sans

CONTENT STRUCTURE AND VISUAL LOGIC

The originators of HTML were scientists who wanted a standard means to share particle physics documents. They had little interest in the exact visual form of the document as seen on the computer screen. In fact, HTML was designed to enforce a clean separation of content structure and graphic design. The intent was to create a World Wide Web of pages that will display in every system and browser available, including browsers that "read" Web page text to visually impaired users and can be accurately interpreted by automated search and analysis engines.

In casting aside the graphic design and editorial management traditions of publishing, the original designers of the Web ignored human motivation. They were so concerned about making Web documents machine-friendly that they produced documents that only machines (or particle physicists) would want to read. In focusing solely on the structural logic of documents they ignored the need for the visual logic of sophisticated graphic design and typography.

For example, most graphic designers avoid using the standard heading tags in HTML (H1, H2, and so on) because they lack subtlety: in most Web browsers these tags make headlines look absurdly large (H1, H2) or ridiculously small (H4, H5, H6). But the header tags in HTML were not created with graphic design in mind. Their sole purpose is to designate a hierarchy of headline importance, so that both human readers and automated search engines can look at a document and easily determine its information structure.

Only incidentally did browser designers create a visual hierarchy for HTML headers by assigning different type sizes and levels of boldness to each header element.

CASCADING STYLE SHEETS

This division between structural logic and visual logic is on its way to being reconciled through the use of Cascading Style Sheets (CSS). Style sheets provide control over the exact visual style of headers, paragraphs, lists, and other page elements. For example, if you prefer H3 headers to be set in 12-point Arial bold type, you can specify those details in a style sheet. In this way you can retain the logical use of HTML's structural tags without sacrificing graphic design flexibility.

At this writing, however, the major Web browsers offer inconsistent and incomplete CSS support. Although both Microsoft Internet Explorer version 3.0 and higher and Netscape Navigator version 4.0 and higher *support* CSS,

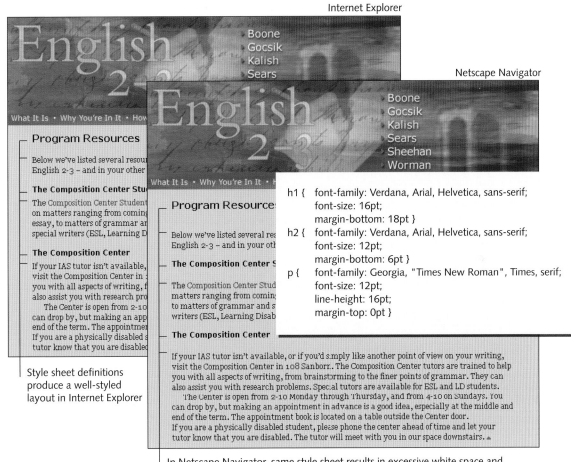

Internet Explorer

Netscape Navigator

```
h1 {   font-family: Verdana, Arial, Helvetica, sans-serif;
       font-size: 16pt;
       margin-bottom: 18pt }
h2 {   font-family: Verdana, Arial, Helvetica, sans-serif;
       font-size: 12pt;
       margin-bottom: 6pt }
p {    font-family: Georgia, "Times New Roman", Times, serif;
       font-size: 12pt;
       line-height: 16pt;
       margin-top: 0pt }
```

Style sheet definitions produce a well-styled layout in Internet Explorer

In Netscape Navigator, same style sheet results in excessive white space and headings that "float" above paragraphs their exact implementations of it differ. A most frustrating example of this is the margin property. Standard HTML headings float far above the paragraphs they describe. With style sheets authors can designate more suitable margins in a heading style declaration. Yet the Netscape browser *adds* the designated amount *to the standard margin*, whereas Explorer simply adds the margin defined in the style sheet. The upshot is that until the browsers offer a more consistent implementation of CSS, only a handful of properties can be used reliably.

So what do you do when you know the advantages of preserving the document structure but you want to design Web pages that are attractive and functional enough to capture and sustain an audience? You compromise. In the sites we create we use a grab bag of tricks to present as polished and sophisticated a page design as we can manage within the boundaries of "official" HTML. We use no proprietary HTML tags, such as those specific to Internet Explorer or Netscape Navigator. Our approach to typography emphasizes visual design over structural purity. Wherever possible, we use "plain vanilla" HTML to describe document structure and CSS to define visual layout. We do not strive for complete control and consistency for our pages but instead accept a certain degree of variability between platforms and browsers. Where CSS falls short, however, we dip into our grab bag of tricks rather than sacrifice visual integrity. We believe that this is the best compromise until everyone can shift over to a mature implementation of CSS and leave plain HTML behind.

Advantages of CSS   This book is not a manual on HTML, and covering the full design implications of Cascading Style Sheets is well beyond the scope of this chapter. If you are not using CSS to manage the graphic design of your Web site, however, you should at least be planning a transition to CSS technology within the next year.

Cascading Style Sheets offer Web designers two key advantages in managing complex Web sites:

- Separation of content and design. CSS gives site developers the best of both worlds: content markup that reflects the logical structure of the information and the freedom to specify exactly how each HTML tag will look.
- Efficient control over large document sets. The most powerful implementations of CSS will allow site designers to control the graphic "look and feel" of thousands of pages by modifying a single master style sheet document.

Style sheets provide greater typographic control with less code. Using plain HTML, you need to define the physical properties of an element such as the <H1> tag each time you use it.

```
<H1 ALIGN="center"><FONT FACE="Verdana, Helvetica, Arial, sans-serif"
SIZE="6" COLOR="gray">Section heading</H1>
```

When you define these properties using CSS, that single definition, or *rule*, applies to every instance of the <H1> element in all documents that reference the style sheet.

> H1 { text-align: center; font-size: 16pt; font-family: Verdana, Helvetica, Arial, sans-serif; color: gray }

In addition, style sheets offer more formatting options than plain HTML tags and extensions. For example, interline spacing, or *leading*, can be controlled using style sheets, as can such text properties as letterspacing and background color. And fortunately the text formatting properties are implemented well enough across browsers to be used with some consistency.

How style sheets work   Style sheets are not new. Every graphic Web browser (even back to Mosaic 1.0) has incorporated style sheets. It just wasn't possible to modify the fixed styles that browsers used to determine, for example, exactly how H1 headers look on the screen. The fundamental idea behind CSS is to let site authors and users determine the size, style, and layout details for each standard HTML tag.

If you have ever used the "styles" features of a page layout or word processing program, you will understand the basic idea behind CSS. The styles feature of a word processor is used to determine exactly how your titles, subheadings, and body copy will look, and then the copy is formatted when you apply a style to each element. Once all the copy has been styled, you can change the look of each occurrence of every element simply by changing the style information. CSS works in the same way, except that with CSS you can set up one master style sheet that will control the visual styling of every page in your site that is linked to the master style sheet:

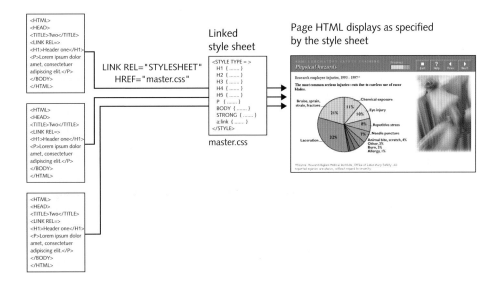

LEGIBILITY

Good typography depends on the visual contrast between one font and another and between text blocks, headlines, and the surrounding white space. Nothing attracts the eye and brain of the reader like strong contrast and distinctive patterns, and you can achieve those attributes only by carefully designing them into your pages. If you cram every page with dense text, readers see a wall of gray and will instinctively reject the lack of visual contrast. Just making things uniformly bigger doesn't help. Even boldface fonts quickly become monotonous, because if everything is bold then nothing stands out "boldly."

When your content is primarily text, typography is the tool you use to "paint" patterns of organization on the page. The first thing the reader sees is not the title or other details on the page but the overall pattern and contrast of the page. The regular, repeating patterns established through carefully organized pages of text and graphics help the reader to establish the location and organization of your information and increase legibility. Patchy, heterogeneous typography and text headers make it hard for the user to see repeating patterns and almost impossible to predict where information is likely to be located in unfamiliar documents:

Too patchy, inconsistent

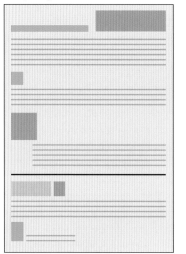

Better layout of type blocks

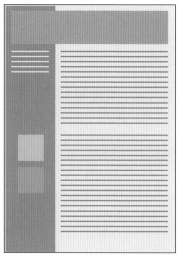

ALIGNMENT

Margins define the reading area of your page by separating the main text from the surrounding environment. Margins provide important visual relief in any document, but careful design of margins and other "white space" is particularly important in Web page design because Web content must coexist on the computer screen with the interface elements of the browser itself and with other windows, menus, and icons of the user interface.

Web content must share the screen with other user interface elements

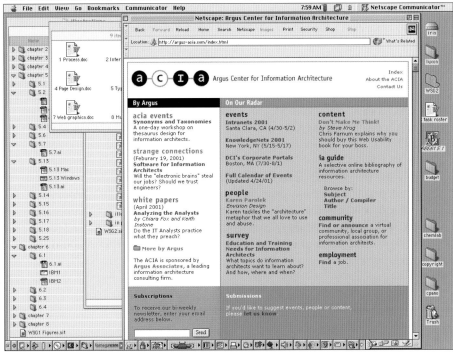

Margins and space can be used to delineate the main text from the other page elements. And when used consistently, margins provide unity throughout a site by creating a consistent structure and look to the site pages. They also add visual interest by contrasting the positive space of the screen (text, graphics) from the negative (white) space.

Text blocks have different ways of sitting within margins. Left-justified, centered, right-justified, and justified text are the alignment options available on the Web.

Justified text   Justified text is set flush with the left and right margins. Justified blocks of text create solid rectangles, and block headings are normally centered for a symmetrical, formal-looking document. In print, justification is achieved by adjusting the space between words and by using word hyphenation. Page layout programs use a hyphenation dictionary to check for and apply hyphenation at each line's end and then adjust word spacing throughout the line. But even with sophisticated page layout software, justified text blocks often suffer from poor spacing and excessive hyphenation and require manual refinement. This level of control is not even a remote possibility on Web pages. The most recent browser versions (and css) support justified text, but it is achieved by crude adjustments to word spacing. Fine adjustments are not possible on low-resolution computer displays and are impractical to implement in today's Web browsers. Also, Web browsers are unlikely to offer automatic hyphenation any time soon, another "must" for properly justified text. For the foreseeable future, the legibility of your Web documents will suffer if you set your text in justified format.

Centered and right-justified text blocks Centered and right-justified text blocks are difficult to read. We read from left to right, anchoring our tracking across the page at the vertical line of the left margin. The ragged left margins produced by centering or right-justifying text make that scanning much harder, because your eye needs to search for the beginning of each new line.

Left-justified text Left-justified text is the most legible option for Web pages because the left margin is even and predictable and the right margin is irregular. Unlike justified text, left justification requires no adjustment to word spacing; the inequities in spacing fall at the end of the lines. The resulting "ragged" right margin adds variety and interest to the page without interfering with legibility.

Left-justified, ragged right	Centered, ragged left and right	Right-justified, ragged left

A ragged left margin makes for difficult reading

Justification of headlines Titles and headings over left-justified body text should also be flush left. Centered headings pair well with justified text, but justified text should not be used on Web pages. Centered display type contrasts with the asymmetry of the ragged right margin of left-justified body text and produces an unbalanced page.

Until typographic options for Web pages become more sophisticated, we recommend that you use left-justified text blocks and headlines as the best solution for most layout situations.

LINE LENGTH

Text on the computer screen is hard to read not only because of the low resolution of computer screens but also because the layout of most Web pages violates a fundamental rule of book and magazine typography: the lines of text on most Web pages are far too long for easy reading. Magazine and book columns are narrow for physiological reasons: at normal reading distances the eye's span of acute focus is only about three inches wide, so designers try to keep dense passages of text in columns not much wider than that comfortable eye span. Wider lines of text require readers to move their heads slightly or strain their eye muscles to track over the long lines of text. Readability suffers because on the long trip back to the left margin the reader may lose track of the next line.

You can use invisible tables (BORDER="0") to restrict the text line length to about fifty to seventy characters per line (see Chapter 4, *Page layout*). The exact character count is difficult to predict because of the way different browser software and operating systems display type sizes. In conventional print layouts, columns of thirty to forty characters per line are considered ideal.

In the end, the decision to restrict line length is a philosophical one. From a design standpoint, a measure that is comfortable for reading is good practice. One of the fundamental principles of the Web, however, is that users should be able to structure their own view. Users with a large monitor may not want their text blocks circumscribed if it means that a large portion of their screen goes unused. A low-vision user with fonts set large will not appreciate being forced to view long pages with short lines of text. So although leaving text free to fill the browser window may affect readability, following conventions may also affect the accessibility and legibility of your documents.

Fixed text block, large portion of the screen unused

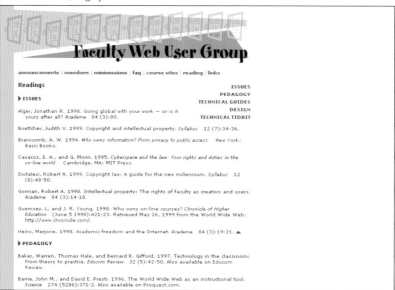

Unrestricted text fills browser window, long lines of text

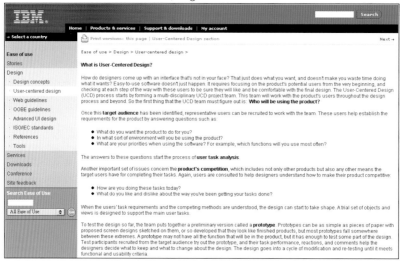

When designing a fixed-width layout, we typically use page layout tables with text cells no wider than about 365 pixels. If 12-point Times New Roman type is used, this cell width yields a line about fifty characters long, averaging about nine to ten words per line. We believe that this achieves the best balance between space efficiency and legibility. If you choose a flexible layout approach, use css leading controls to increase line spacing to 15 or 16 points (see *White space*, below). Additional line spacing allows a somewhat longer line length without sacrificing legibility.

WHITE SPACE

The vertical space in a text block is called leading, and it is the distance from one baseline of text to the next. Leading strongly affects the legibility of text blocks: too much leading makes it hard for the eye to locate the start of the next line, whereas too little leading confuses the lines of type, because the ascenders of one line get jumbled with the descenders of the line above. In plain HTML it is not possible to implement true leading, but css offers leading control (referred to as "line spacing" in css terminology). In print one general rule is to set the leading of text blocks at about 2 points above the size of the type. For example, 12-point type could be set with 14 points of leading. We suggest generous leading to compensate for longer line lengths and the lower resolution of the computer screen, for example, 12-point type with 14 to 16 points of leading.

Indenting paragraphs   There are two major schools of thought on denoting paragraphs. The classic typographic method uses indents to signal the beginning of a new paragraph (as we have in this book). However, many technical, reference, and trade publications now use a blank line of white space to separate paragraphs. Indented paragraphs work especially well for longer blocks of prose, where the indents signal new paragraphs with minimal disruption to the flow of text. Blank line spacing between paragraphs, in contrast, makes a page easy to scan and provides extra white space for visual relief. Either approach is valid as long as the paragraph style is implemented consistently throughout the site.

To indent paragraphs without using css, you can insert several nonbreaking space characters ( ) at the start of each paragraph. You can also use a transparent single-pixel GIF graphic as a spacer and adjust its horizontal spacing. If you are using css you can set the exact spacing for the indentation using the "text-indent" property of paragraphs.

```
     To indent paragraphs without using css,…
<IMG SRC="pixel.gif" HEIGHT="1" WIDTH ="1" ALT="" HSPACE="8">
To indent paragraphs without using css,…
<P STYLE="text-indent: 8pt"> To indent paragraphs without using css,…
```

To separate paragraphs with blank lines you could put a paragraph tag (<P>) at the end of each paragraph. The paragraph tag adds a full blank line between paragraphs. To adjust the amount to an amount less or more than a full blank line you can use the css "margin" property, but beware of spacing inconsistencies between browsers. You can also use the line break tag (<BR>) followed by a transparent single-pixel GIF graphic as a spacer to control the space between paragraphs. As always when using a spacer graphic, be sure to include empty ALT text to hide the image from assistive technologies and text-only browsers:

```
<BR>
<IMG SRC="pixel.gif" HEIGHT="1" WIDTH ="1" ALT="" VSPACE="2">
```

TYPEFACES

Each typeface has a unique tone that should produce a harmonious fit between the verbal and visual flow of your content. With the first versions of HTML, Web authors had no control over typefaces ("fonts" in personal computer terminology). Fonts were set by the browser, so pages were viewed in whatever font the user specified in his or her browser preferences. The more recent versions of HTML and css allow designers to specify the typeface. This is useful not only for aesthetic reasons but also because of the differing dimensions of typefaces. A layout that is carefully designed using one face may not format correctly in another.

In specifying typefaces you should choose from the resident default fonts for most operating systems. If you specify a font that is not on the user's machine, the browser will display your pages using the user-specified default font. Bear in mind, too, that users can set their browser preferences to ignore font tags and display all pages using their designated default font.

Legibility on screen   Some typefaces are more legible than others on the screen. A traditional typeface such as Times Roman is considered to be one of the most legible on paper, but at screen resolution its size is too small and its shapes look irregular. Screen legibility is most influenced by the x-height (the height of a lowercase "x") and the overall size of the typeface.

Adapted traditional typefaces   Times New Roman is a good example of a traditional typeface that has been adapted for use on computer screens. A serif typeface like Times New Roman (the default text face in most Web browsers) is about average in legibility on the computer screen, with a moderate x-height. Times New Roman is a good font to use in text-heavy documents that will probably be printed by readers rather than read from the screen. The compact letter size of Times New Roman also makes it a good choice if you need to pack a lot of words into a small space.

Designed for the screen   Typefaces such as Georgia and Verdana were designed specifically for legibility on the computer screen; they have exaggerated x-heights and are very large compared to more traditional typefaces in the same point size. These fonts offer excellent legibility for Web pages designed to be read directly from the screen. However, the exaggerated x-heights and heavy letterforms of these fonts look massive and clumsy when transferred to the high-resolution medium of paper.

Choosing typefaces   The most conventional scheme for using typefaces is to use a serif face such as Times New Roman or Georgia for body text and a sans serif face such as Verdana or Arial as a contrast for headlines. We generally set our text-laden Web pages in Times New Roman because it produces a reasonable balance between density of information and overall legibility. Most readers expect a serif font for long blocks of text and find Times New Roman comfortable to read off-screen from paper printouts. Various studies purport to show that serif type is more legible than sans serif type and vice versa. You can truly judge type legibility only within the context of the situation—on the screen—as users will see your Web page.

You may use either a variation of the serif font or a contrasting sans serif face for the display type. It is safest to use a single typographic family and vary its weight and size for display type and emphasis. If you choose to combine serif and sans serif faces, select fonts that are compatible and don't use more than two typefaces (one serif, one sans serif) on a page.

The most useful fonts that ship with the Apple Macintosh and Microsoft Windows operating systems are reproduced here (we have omitted bitmap fonts and decorative or novelty typefaces):

Windows

Times New Roman
Each typeface has a unique tone that should produce a harmonious fit between the verbal and visual flow of your content.

Georgia
Each typeface has a unique tone that should produce a harmonious fit between the verbal and visual flow of your content.

Verdana
Each typeface has a unique tone that should produce a harmonious fit between the verbal and visual flow of your content.

Arial
Each typeface has a unique tone that should produce a harmonious fit between the verbal and visual flow of your content.

Trebuchet
Each typeface has a unique tone that should produce a harmonious fit between the verbal and visual flow of your content.

Macintosh

Times New Roman
Each typeface has a unique tone that should produce a harmonious fit between the verbal and visual flow of your content.

Georgia
Each typeface has a unique tone that should produce a harmonious fit between the verbal and visual flow of your content.

Verdana
Each typeface has a unique tone that should produce a harmonious fit between the verbal and visual flow of your content.

Arial
Each typeface has a unique tone that should produce a harmonious fit between the verbal and visual flow of your content.

Trebuchet
Each typeface has a unique tone that should produce a harmonious fit between the verbal and visual flow of your content.

Specifying typefaces The early versions of HTML did not allow designers to specify a typeface for Web documents. With version 3.2 came several new tags aimed at giving designers more control over the visual properties of elements, among them the FONT tag. Many of these have been "deprecated" by the World Wide Web Consortium, which means that they may be dropped from future versions of HTML. Although the added tags enable designers to create more elegant-looking pages, they also result in cumbersome code that is difficult to adapt and maintain. You *can* still use the FONT tag to set the type in your documents, but a better approach is to consolidate text formatting in style sheets.

You can specify any typeface for your Web pages, but many computers have only the default operating system fonts installed. If the typeface you specify is not available on the user's computer, the browser will switch to the default font (generally "Times New Roman" or "Times"). To increase the chances that the reader will see a typeface you are happy with, you can specify multiple fonts. The browser will check for the presence of each font (in the order given), so you can specify three or four alternates before the browser applies the default font, for example, "Verdana, Geneva, Arial, Helvetica." As a last-ditch effort you can end your font declaration with a generic font designation such as "sans serif." That way, if the browser cannot find any of the listed fonts, it will display the text in any available sans serif font.

```
P { font-family: "Times New Roman", Georgia, Times, serif }
```

Notice that multiword fonts like "Times New Roman" must appear within quotation marks.

A good way to make sure that your type settings are functioning correctly is to set your browser's default proportional font setting to something that is obviously different from your intended font. For example, set your browser's default font to Courier if you are not using Courier in your document. When you view your page, anything that appears in Courier must not be marked up properly.

TYPE SIZE

Setting the size of type is a matter of some controversy. The Web is supposed to be a universal medium where users of all kinds have equal access to information. As opposed to a printed medium, where the layout and type are fixed, Web pages should adapt to meet the needs of all comers, so that, for example, low-vision users can set the type of Web documents to display at a size that they find legible. But these adjustments can skew a page layout and send the designer, who diligently designed the page around a specific size of type, into paroxysms. And though variation thwarts the designer who worked to fashion the layout, it is undeniable that the low-vision user *ought* to be able to gain access to the content.

With the introduction of the FONT tag, designers also gained the ability to set the font size. With css, designers have many methods for setting type size, although, as with many other css properties, all are not fully supported. The w3c recommends that you let users set the base font size in their browser and that you set all variations using the "em" unit. An em in the Web context is the same as the font height, which makes it a relative unit and therefore flexible. For example, if the user-set default is 12-point, then a 2-em text indent would be 24-point, but if the user used the text zoom feature of the browser to change the size to 16-point, the indent would change to 32-point to reflect the larger type size.

```
P { font-family: Verdana, Arial, Helvetica, sans-serif; font-size: 1em; text-indent: 2em }
```

As you might imagine, this flexibility can send page layouts into disarray. If you try this approach, use a flexible page layout that will hold up to large type.

With a well-designed flexible layout, the design remains intact even when the text is enlarged

You can also use points to define your type sizes, but bear in mind that this carryover from the print medium has little meaning on a computer screen. Because monitors display at different resolutions, 12-point type on one screen could approximate 14-point type on another. This can be particularly problematic for small point sizes. For example, 6-point type is legible on a Windows display, where the default resolution is 96 ppi, but on a Macintosh, at 72 ppi, it is illegible.

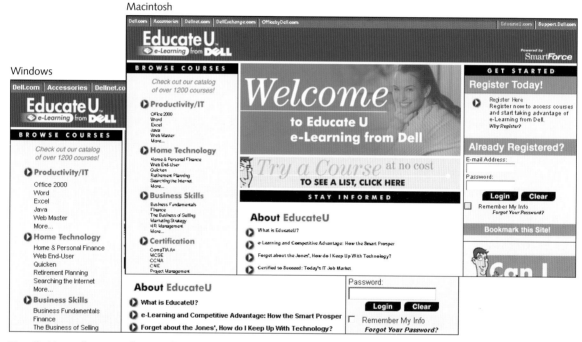

Type that is small on a Windows machine can be totally illegible on a Macintosh

Still, points are familiar and, though variable, offer some means of declaring the relative size of type elements.

```
H1 { font-family: Verdana, Arial, Helvetica, sans-serif; font-size: 14 pt }
P { font-family: Georgia, "Times New Roman", Times, serif; font-size: 12 pt }
```

Just remember that declaring your type in points does not mean that the point size you specify is what will actually display on the user's monitor. And because this unit is not "fixed"—that is, type set in points can be resized in the browser—this approach also requires an adaptable layout.

If the integrity of your layout depends on specific type sizes, the most dependable option right now—until there is better CSS support—is to use pixel units in your style declarations. Text defined using pixels will be the same size regardless of the browser's default font size and resolution settings.

P { font-family: Georgia, "Times New Roman", serif; font-size: 12px }

Although this option does offer more stability, be aware that you may be shutting out those users who have good reasons for specifying different font settings.

CASE

Whether you choose uppercase or lowercase letters has a strong effect on the legibility of your text. Indeed, words set in all uppercase letters should generally be avoided—except perhaps for short headings—because they are difficult to scan.

We read primarily by recognizing the overall shape of words, not by parsing each letter and then assembling a recognizable word:

Tree   Boy   Dog

Words formed with capital letters are monotonous rectangles that offer few distinctive shapes to catch the eye:

MONOTONOUS   Monotonous
RECTANGLES   rectangles

We recommend downstyle typing (capitalize only the first word and any proper nouns) for your headlines, subheads, and text. Downstyle is more legible because as we read we primarily scan the tops of words:

Notice how much harder it is to read the bottom half of the same sentence:

If you use initial capital letters in your headlines, you disrupt the reader's scanning of the word forms:

Initial Caps Cause Pointless Bumps

A Web page of solid body text is hard to scan for content structure and will not engage the eye. Adding display type to a document will provide landmarks to direct the reader through your content. Display type establishes an information structure and adds visual variety to draw the reader into your material. The key to effective display type is the careful and economic use of typographic emphasis.

There are time-honored typographical devices for adding emphasis to a block of text, but be sure to use them sparingly. If you make everything bold, then nothing will stand out and it will seem as if you are shouting at your readers. A good rule of thumb when working with type is to add emphasis using one parameter at a time. If you want to draw attention to the section heads in your document, don't set them large, bold, and all caps. If you want them to be larger, increase their size by one measure. If you prefer bold, leave the heads the same size as your body text and make them bold. You will soon discover that only a small variation is required to establish visual contrast.

Italics   Italicized text attracts the eye because it contrasts in shape from body text. Use italics for convention—when listing book or periodical titles, for example—or within text for stressed or foreign words or phrases. Avoid setting large blocks of text in italics because the readability of italicized text, particularly at screen resolutions, is much lower than in comparably sized roman text.

Bold   Boldface text gives emphasis because it contrasts in color from the body text. Section subheads work well set in bold. Boldface text is readable on-screen, though large blocks of text set in bold lack contrast and therefore lose their effectiveness.

Underlined   Underlined text is a carryover from the days of the typewriter, when such options as italics and boldface were unavailable. In addition to its aesthetic shortcomings (too heavy, interferes with letter shapes), underlining has a special functional meaning in Web documents. Most readers have their browser preferences set to underline links. This default browser setting ensures that people with monochromatic monitors or people who are color-blind can identify links within text blocks. If you include underlined text on your Web page it will certainly be confused with a hypertext link.

Colored text   Although the use of color is another option for differentiating type, colored text, like underlining, has a special functional meaning in Web documents. You should avoid putting colored text within text blocks because readers will assume that the colored text is a hypertext link and click on it. Colored text does work well as a subtle means to distinguish section heads, however. Choose dark shades of color that contrast with the page background, and avoid using colors close to the default Web link colors of blue and violet.

Capital letters   Capitalized text is one of the most common and least effective methods for adding typographical emphasis. We recognize words in two ways, by parsing letter groups and by recognizing word shapes. Words or headlines set in all capital letters form rectangles with no distinctive shape. To read a block of text set in all capital letters we must parse the letter groups—read the text letter by letter—which is uncomfortable and significantly slows reading. As you read the following paragraph, notice how tiring the process is:

> THE DESIGN OF THE SITE WILL DETERMINE THE ORGANIZATIONAL FRAMEWORK OF YOUR WEB SITE. AT THIS STAGE YOU WILL MAKE THE ESSENTIAL DECISIONS ABOUT WHAT YOUR AUDIENCE WANTS FROM YOU, WHAT YOU WISH TO SAY, AND HOW TO ARRANGE THE CONTENT TO BEST MEET YOUR AUDIENCE'S NEEDS. ALTHOUGH PEOPLE WILL INSTANTLY NOTICE THE GRAPHIC DESIGN OF YOUR WEB PAGES, THE ORGANIZATION OF THE SITE WILL HAVE THE GREATEST IMPACT ON THEIR EXPERIENCE.

Spacing and indentation   One of the most effective and subtle ways to vary the visual contrast and relative importance of a piece of text is simply to isolate it or treat it differently from the surrounding text. If you want your major headers to stand out more without making them larger, add space before the header to separate it from any previous copy. Indentation is another effective means of distinguishing bulleted lists, quotations, or example text (such as the capitalization example above). HTML lists are automatically indented (too far, in our estimation), and you can use the BLOCKQUOTE tag to indent blocks of text. You can define your own indents using CSS.

Advantages of CSS

This book is not a manual on HTML, and covering the full design implications of Cascading Style Sheets is well beyond the scope of this chapter. If you are not using CSS to manage the graphic design of your Web site, however, you should at least be planning a transition to CSS technology within the next year.

Cascading Style Sheets offer Web designers

- Separation of content and design. CSS
  markup that reflects the logical struc
  how each HTML tag will look.
- Efficient control over large documen
  site designers to control the graphic
  master style sheet document.

Style sheets provide greater typographic c
the physical properties of an element such

```
<H1 ALIGN="center"><FONT FACE
SIZE="6" COLOR="gray">Section
```

When you define these properties using C
the <H1> element in all documents that re

```
H1 { text-align: right; font-
Arial, sans-serif; color: gra
```

Advantages of CSS

This book is not a manual on HTML, and covering the full design implications of Cascading Style Sheets is well beyond the scope of this chapter. If you are not using CSS to manage the graphic design of your Web site, however, you should at least be planning a transition to CSS technology within the next year.

Cascading Style Sheets offer Web designers two key advantages in managing complex Web sites:

- Separation of content and design. CSS gives site developers the best of both worlds: content markup that reflects the logical structure of the information and the freedom to specify exactly how each HTML tag will look.
- Efficient control over large document sets. The most powerful implementations of CSS will allow site designers to control the graphic "look and feel" of thousands of pages by modifying a single master style sheet document.

Style sheets provide greater typographic control with less code. Using plain HTML, you need to define the physical properties of an element such as the <H1> tag each time you use it.

```
<H1 ALIGN="center"><FONT FACE="Verdana, Helvetica, Arial, sans-serif" SIZE="6" COLOR="gray">
Section heading</H1>
```

When you define these properties using CSS, that single definition, or rule, applies to every instance of the <H1> element in all documents that reference the style sheet.

```
H1 { text-align: right; font-size: 16pt; font-family: Verdana, Helvetica, Arial, sans-serif; color: gray }
```

CONSISTENCY

As in traditional print publishing, high-quality Web sites adhere to established type style settings consistently throughout the site. Consistency gives polish to a site and encourages visitors to stay by creating an expectation about the structure of a text. If sloppy, inconsistent formatting confounds this expectation, you will confuse your readers and they may not return.

You should decide on such settings as fonts, inter-paragraph spacing, the size of subheads, and so on and then create a written style guide to help you maintain these settings as you develop the site. This step is especially critical for large sites that incorporate numerous pages.

If you choose to use CSS you will have powerful tools to maintain the consistency of styles throughout your site. This is particularly true if you opt to use a master style sheet for your whole site via the "Link" option in CSS (see *Cascading Style Sheets*, above).

CROSS-PLATFORM ISSUES

RELATIVE FONT SIZES

The Macintosh and Windows operating systems display type differently, even when the same typefaces are being used. In general, type displayed on Windows Web browsers will look 2 to 3 points larger than the equivalent face on the Macintosh. Thus a line of 12-point Times type on a Macintosh looks more like 14 points in Times New Roman on a Windows machine. This difference in font rendering can have a big impact on your page layouts. The following table shows the major Microsoft TrueType typefaces in their 12-point sizes, as displayed in both Windows and on a Macintosh.

Windows	Macintosh
Arial	Arial
Courier	Courier
Georgia	Georgia
Times New Roman	Times New Roman
Trebuchet MS	Trebuchet
Verdana	Verdana

If you don't have ready access to a machine with "the other" operating system and you use Netscape Navigator, you can use Netscape's "Preferences/Fonts" box to change the default text size from 12 to 14 (Mac users) or from 12 to 11 or 10 (Windows users). If you use Internet Explorer you can use the "Larger" or "Smaller" controls on the button bar to manipulate the default font size of the text.

The basic fonts that come with Windows and the Macintosh operating system are listed below. If you are going to specify fonts for your Web documents, you should probably use the typefaces listed here, and you should always specify at least one typeface from each operating system (for example: "Arial, Geneva") to avoid having the browser render your pages in the default font:

Windows	Macintosh
Arial	**Charcoal**
Courier	**Chicago**
Courier New	Courier
MS Sans Serif	Geneva
MS Serif	Helvetica
Times New Roman	Monaco
Verdana	New York
	Palatino
	Times

Remember that many Macintosh users who have installed Microsoft Office or Microsoft's Internet Explorer Web browser will have "Windows" fonts installed on their systems. If you specify the fonts "Georgia, Times" in your font definitions, many Macintosh users will see their text set in Georgia, just as Windows users do.

Also note in the relative font sizes example on the preceding page that although "Trebuchet" and "Trebuchet MS" are basically the same typeface, the exact name you specify in the font list matters. If you want both Macintosh and Windows users to see the typeface Trebuchet, then use both names in your font declaration.

ACCESSIBILITY

When considering type, the main accessibility issues are size and color. These attributes come into play for users who have vision disabilities such as low vision or color blindness. Vision-impaired users need to be able to transform text that they find illegible into a format that they can read. Low-vision users need to be able to increase the type size and set the text and page background colors for maximum contrast. Colorblind users also need control over text and background color. You need to pay attention to the following type and layout attributes to accommodate users with vision disabilities.

Scalable text   Users cannot easily enlarge text that is set using absolute size values, for example, text sized using pixels (see *Type size*, above). To ensure scalability, use relative units such as the em unit to control the typography—type size, margins and indents, leading—on the page. Use text graphics sparingly, and always offer a text-only equivalent. Text rendered to graphic form is no longer text but image and cannot be manipulated—enlarged, colored—as plain text can.

Structural markup   Text formatting done using presentation-style markup instead of style sheets limits users' ability to transform a layout to meet their needs. Some browsers have a feature that allows users to override author-defined style sheets with their own style sheet. This means that users can define a custom style sheet that meets their viewing needs. For example, a low-vision user might define a style sheet that renders all <P> text at 24 points, or a colorblind user might set the background to white and the text to black for maximum contrast. But these measures will not work, or will only work partially, on pages that are formatted using presentation markup. If text color is set using <FONT COLOR> and headings are set using <FONT SIZE> and <B> for emphasis, the user-defined style sheet will have nothing to apply itself to (no paragraph or heading tags). If you set presentation properties using style sheets, users who *need* to customize the page can do so.

Emphasis   If you use color alone to achieve typographic emphasis, users who cannot distinguish the colors will miss the emphasis. To emphasize text—for example, in headers or key phrases within text—so that it won't be overlooked, use bold formatting as well as color. (Indeed, colored text for anything that is not a link is a potential usability flaw that you might as well avoid altogether. See *Colored text*, above.) Also be sure that there is sufficient contrast between the background and text on your page. Although contrast is particularly important for vision-impaired users, all users will benefit from greater readability.

Adaptable layouts   Most Web page layouts are not designed with large type in mind. For example, fixed layouts that limit the text column to a specified width are typically sized to accommodate 12-point type or smaller. Indeed, at large type sizes a fixed text column may contain only a few words, which makes the text awkward to read. For adaptable pages, use a flexible layout that transforms gracefully to accommodate larger type sizes. (For more on fixed and flexible layouts, see Chapter 4, *Page layout*.)

TYPE GRAPHICS

Typography cannot always be neatly separated from the graphics of your Web site. Graphic text can be tightly integrated with images in ways that are impossible in HTML text:

For aesthetic reasons you may choose to use graphical representations of type rather than manipulate HTML type. In either case you'll need to understand how to best render type within GIF (Graphics Interchange Format) and JPEG (Joint Photographic Experts Group) graphics.

ANTIALIASED TYPE

Antialiasing is a technique widely used in computer graphics to optimize the look of graphics and typography on the display screen. Antialiasing visually "smoothes" the shapes in graphics and type by inserting pixels of intermediate colors along boundary edges between colors. In typography, antialiasing removes the jagged edges of larger type characters. At normal viewing distances antialiasing gives the impression that the type is rendered at a higher resolution:

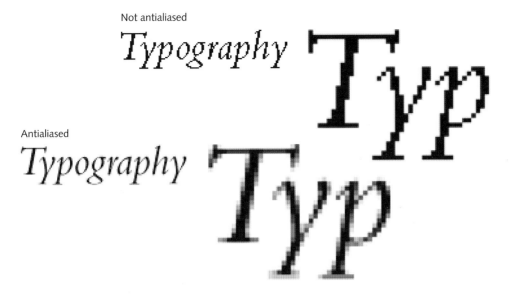

Not antialiased

Typography

Antialiased

Typography

Creating antialiased type Sophisticated image editing programs such as Adobe Photoshop will create antialiased type automatically, and these "paint" image editors are where most Web designers create their graphic typography. If, however, you have a complex arrangement of typography and graphics (say, for a home page banner), you may wish to work first in a drawing program such as Adobe Illustrator or Macromedia FreeHand. Drawing programs are better at laying out text and will let you edit the text up to the final rendering into a paint (GIF or JPEG) graphic to use on the Web page. Final rendering is usually done by importing the graphic into Photoshop, where all text will automatically become antialiased:

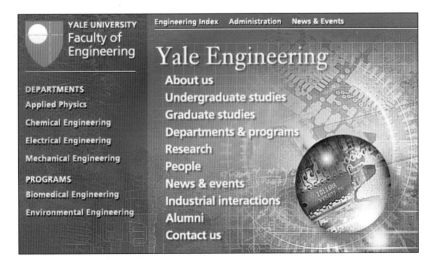

We often use graphic type within banner or navigational graphics, but we rarely use graphic type simply as a stylistic substitute for headlines or subheads within a Web page. Purely graphic typography cannot be searched and indexed along with the HTML-based text on a Web page. Your best option is to repeat the textual content of the graphic inside an ALT tag and hope that search engines will pick up that content, too. Finally, bear in mind that graphic type is far more difficult to edit or update than HTML text.

When not to use antialiasing   Antialiasing is great for large display type, but it is not suitable for small type sizes, especially type smaller than 10 points. The antialiasing reduces the legibility of small type, particularly when you import it into Photoshop from a drawing program like Adobe Illustrator. If you need to antialias small type sizes, do it in Photoshop:

	Search	Home	Comments	Index	
Geneva	Search	Home	Comments	Index	Type not antialiased
Arial	Search	Home	Comments	Index	Set in Microsoft Word
Times New Roman	Search	Home	Comments	Index	and captured as a screen grab
Georgia	Search	Home	Comments	Index	

	Search	Home	Comments	Index	
Geneva	Search	Home	Comments	Index	Type set in Adobe Illustrator and
Arial	Search	Home	Comments	Index	imported into Adobe Photoshop
Times New Roman	Search	Home	Comments	Index	with antialiasing on (Results are poor for small
Georgia	Search	Home	Comments	Index	type sizes; avoid doing this)

	Search	Home	Comments	Index	
Geneva	Search	Home	Comments	Index	Type set in Adobe Photoshop
Arial	Search	Home	Comments	Index	with antialiasing on
Times New Roman	Search	Home	Comments	Index	Best results for small
Georgia	Search	Home	Comments	Index	antialiased type sizes

For the anatomic illustration below we used non-antialiased 9-point Geneva (a Macintosh screen font) for the illustration labels:

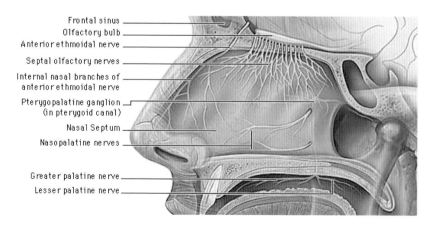

REFERENCES

Brewer, Judy, ed. 2001. *How people with disabilities use the Web*. http://www.w3c.org/WAI/EO/Drafts/PWD-Use-Web (31 March 2001).

Bringhurst, Robert. 1996. *The elements of typographic style*, 2d ed. Vancouver, B.C.: Hartley and Marks.

Carter, Rob, Ben Day, and Philip Meggs. 1993. *Typographic design: Form and communication*, 2d ed. New York: Van Nostrand Reinhold.

Chisholm, Wendy, Gregg Vanderheiden, and Ian Jacobs, eds. 1999. *Web content accessibility guidelines 1.0*. http://www.w3c.org/TR/WAI-WEBCONTENT/wai-pageauth.html (17 January 2001).

Lie, Håkon Wium, and Bert Bos. 1999. *Cascading Style Sheets: Designing for the Web*, 2d ed. Reading, Mass.: Addison-Wesley.

Microsoft Corporation. 2000. *Microsoft typography*. http://www.microsoft.com/typography/default.asp.

Pring, Roger. 2000. *www.type: Effective typographic design for the World Wide Web*. New York: Watson-Guptill.

Spiekermann, Erik, and E. M. Ginger. 1993. *Stop stealing sheep and find out how type works*. Mountain View, Calif.: Adobe.

Williams, Robin. 1990. *The Mac is not a typewriter: A style manual for creating professional-level type on your Macintosh*. Berkeley, Calif.: Peachpit.

———. 1992. *The PC is not a typewriter: A style manual for creating professional-level type on your personal computer*. Berkeley, Calif.: Peachpit.

Wilson, Adrian. 1993. *The design of books*. San Francisco: Chronicle Books.

6   *Editorial Style*

First we thought the PC was a calculator. Then we found out how
to turn numbers into letters with ASCII—and we thought it was a
typewriter. Then we discovered graphics, and we thought it was
a television. With the World Wide Web, we've realized it's
a brochure.
—Douglas Adams

AMONG THE MANY Web-induced trends, the emergence of a new writing
genre designed to accommodate the reading habits of Web users is especially
notable. People read differently on the Web. One reason for this is that
reading text on-screen is unpleasant. Given the low resolution of the computer screen and the clumsiness of the scrolling page, many readers scan on-
screen and print pages for reading. Another reason is that Web reading is
not a stationary activity. Users roam from page to page collecting salient bits
of information from a variety of sources. They need to be able quickly to as-
certain the contents of a page, get the information they are seeking, and
move on. Also, because Web pages may be accessed directly without preamble, they must be more independent than print pages. Too many Web pages
end up as isolated fragments of information, divorced from the larger context of their parent Web sites through the lack of essential links and the
simpler failure to inform the reader properly of their contents.

One of the most obvious characteristics of Web writing is hypertext
links. Web authors use hypertext links to create or supplement concepts: a
list of related links can reinforce their content or even serve as the focus of
their site. The problem posed by links has little to do with the Web but is
rooted in the concept of hypertext: Can the quick juxtaposition of two separate but conceptually related pieces of information encourage a better understanding of the overall message? A collection of links cannot create or
sustain an argument or deliver a collection of facts as efficiently or legibly as
conventional linear prose. When there is no sustained narrative, readers are
sent aimlessly wandering in their quest for information. Links also become a
maintenance issue, because most Web pages are ephemeral. Broken links
shake the reader's confidence in the validity and timeliness of content.
Links should be used sparingly and as a reinforcement of, not a substitute
for, content.

ORGANIZING YOUR PROSE

Documents written to be read online must be concise and structured for scanning. People tend to skim Web pages rather than read them word by word. Use headings, lists, and typographical emphasis for words or sections you wish to highlight; these are the elements that will grab the user's attention during a quick scan. Keep these elements clear and precise—use your page and section heads to describe the material. The "inverted pyramid" style used in journalism works well on Web pages, with the conclusion appearing at the beginning of a text. Place the important facts near the top of the first paragraph where users can find them quickly.

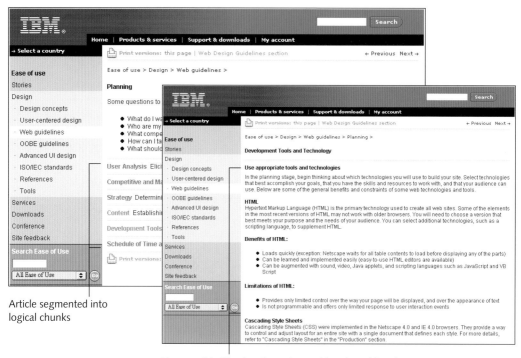

Article segmented into
logical chunks

Typographical landmarks such as subheads and lists for easy scanning

That said, keep in mind that much content is not well suited to the telegraphic style that works well for online documents. Web authors often cut so much out of their presentations that what remains would barely fill a printed pamphlet. Concise writing is always better, but don't "dumb down" what you have to say. You can assume that readers will print anything longer than half a page and read it offline. Simply make printing easy for your readers and you can use the Web to deliver content without cutting the heart out of what you have to say.

Another way to style online documents is to break up your information into logical "chunks" connected by hypertext links, but only where it makes sense (see Chapter 3, *"Chunking" information*). Don't break up a long document arbitrarily; users will have to download each segment and will have difficulty printing or saving the entire piece. The key to good chunking is to divide your information into comprehensive segments. That way readers will have direct and complete access to the topics they are interested in without having to wade through irrelevant material or follow a series of links to get the whole picture.

ONLINE STYLE

For most Web writing you should assume that your carefully crafted prose will not be read word by word. This is *not* the case, of course, for texts such as journal articles or teaching materials: in many cases these more complicated texts will be printed and read offline. But most online information is best presented using short segments of texts written in a clear, concise style and with ample use of editorial landmarks.

PROSE STYLE

Our writing style example below explains the steps involved in creating a successful Web site. The first style is vague and verbose. The second is concise: we simply list the facts. It is this second writing style that is most suitable for Web documents. Most Web readers are looking for information, and they find it not by reading a Web page word by word but rather by scanning the page for relevant items.

Vague and verbose   You must read every word in this paragraph in order to understand the steps involved in creating Web sites:

> Web site development is a complex process that involves many steps and tasks that range from budgeting to design and evaluation. First, you need to define the scope of your project and determine a budget for site development. Then you need to survey and map the structure of your information. The next step is to establish a look and feel for your site, and then comes the actual construction of your site. Once your site is finished you need to make sure people know that it's there and how to find it. Finally, you should spend time evaluating your site's effectiveness. As you embark on the process of developing a Web site, keep these steps in mind and make sure that you have the organizational backing, budget, and personnel you need to make the project a success.

Concise and factual   In this version, we turned the wordy explanation of the process into a concise list of steps to follow:

The process of developing a Web site generally follows these steps:

1 Site definition and budgeting
2 Information architecture
3 Site design
4 Site construction
5 Site marketing
6 Tracking and evaluation

Before beginning to develop a Web site, make sure you have the organizational backing, budget, and personnel you need to perform these steps successfully.

Other stylistic considerations
- Be frugal. Make sure that the text you present is worth something to the reader. Avoid empty chatter like welcome text or instructions on how to use the site. Users should be able to determine who you are by your navigation and page design, and your interface should be clear enough that it doesn't require instructions. Don't use the first paragraph of each page to tell users what information they'll find there. Instead, start with the information, written in the concise and factual prose style shown above.
- Stick to the point. Write in easily understood sentences. Steer clear of clever headings and catchy but meaningless phrases that users must think about and explore further to understand.
- Cultivate a voice. Web readers welcome a *measure* of individuality from their information sources. With so many competing sources, a unique voice may help distinguish your pages, but beware of going "over the top." When it comes to attitude, there is a fine line between engaging and annoying.
- Think globally. Remember that you are designing documents for the *World Wide* Web and that your audience may not understand conventions specific to your little corner of the world. For example, when including dates, use the international date format of day/month/year (e.g., 14 March 2001). Also, avoid metaphors and puns that may make sense only in the context of your language and culture.

TITLES AND SUBTITLES

Editorial landmarks like titles and headers are the fundamental human interface device in Web pages, just as they are in any print publication. A consistent approach to titles, headlines, and subheadings in your documents will help your readers navigate through a complex set of Web pages.

TEXT STYLES

The text styles we recommend:

Headline style: Bold, capitalize initial letters of words
- Document titles
- References to other Web sites
- Titles of documents mentioned in the text
- Proper names, product names, trade names

Down style: Bold, capitalize first word only
- Subheads
- References to other sections within the site
- Figure titles
- Lists

PAGE TITLES

Web page titles are designated in the HTML document head section with the TITLE tag. The title is crucial for several reasons. Often the title is the first thing users with slow Internet connections will see; it also becomes the text for any bookmarks the reader makes to your pages. In addition, most search engines regard the page title as the primary descriptor of page content, so a descriptive title increases the chance that a page will appear as the result of a related search query.

The page title should:

- Incorporate the name of your company, organization, or Web site
- Form a concise, plainly worded reminder of the page contents

Always consider what your page title will look like in a long list of bookmarks. Will the title remind the reader of what he or she found interesting about your pages?

TEXT FORMATTING FOR WEB DOCUMENTS

Some points about text formatting specific to the Web:

Excessive markup   Beware of too much markup in your paragraphs. Too many links or too many styles of typeface will destroy the homogeneous, even "type color" that characterizes good typesetting.

Link colors   If you are including links in the body of your text, choose custom link colors that closely match your text color. Reading from the screen is hard enough without struggling with distracting link colors scattered across the page.

Use the best tool   Write your text in a good word processing program with spell-checking and search features. Transfer your text to HTML only after it has been proofread.

Style sheets in word processors   Don't use the word processor's style sheets to produce "All capitals" or other formatting effects. You will lose those special formats when you convert to plain ASCII text for HTML use.

Special characters   Don't use the "smart quotes" feature. Avoid all special characters, such as bullets, ligatures, and typographer's en and em dashes, that are not supported in standard HTML text. Consult a good HTML guidebook (we recommend several in the References) for the listing of special and international characters supported through HTML's extended character formatting.

No auto hyphens   Never use the automatic hyphenation feature of your word processor on text destined for the Web. This may add nonstandard "optional hyphen" characters that will not display properly in Web browsers.

LINKS

Two basic types of links are used in Web sites: navigational links connect pages within a site and the classic hypertext links offer parenthetical material, footnotes, digressions, or parallel themes that the author believes will enrich the main content of the page. Although navigational links can cause problems in site design, more disruptive is the overuse or poor placement of hypertext links.

Hypertext links pose two fundamental design problems. They disrupt the flow of content in your site by inviting the reader to leave your site. They can also radically alter the context of information by dumping the reader into unfamiliar territory without preamble or explanation.

The primary design strategy in thoughtful hypertext is to use links to reinforce your message, not to distract readers or send them off chasing a minor footnote in some other Web site. Most links in a Web site should point to other resources *within* your site, pages that share the same graphic design, navigational controls, and overall content theme. Whenever possible, integrate related visuals or text materials into your site so that readers do not have the sense that you have dumped them outside your site's framework. If you must send your reader away, make sure the material around the link makes it clear that the reader will be leaving your Web site and entering another site by following the link. Provide a description of the linked site along with the link so users understand the relevance of the linked material.

Links to related materials
listed in page margins

MAINTAIN CONTEXT

The key to good hypertext linking is to *maintain context*, so that the reader stays within the narrative flow and design environment of your site. If you place a simple link on your page, these plain links will work within a single browser window—your content will disappear and the linked page will fill the window. If you use this kind of link to point away from your site, you will probably lose your readers.

The simplest way to maintain context using links to other sites is to add the TARGET="main" argument to your link tags. This will cause the linked page to appear in a new browser window in front of the one containing your page. This feature allows your reader to access new material without losing visual contact with your site.

Opening links in a secondary window allows users to explore related material without losing contact with your site

Frames offer a more complex way to maintain narrative and design context. Using frames you can split the browser screen between your site and the material you wish to bring up with a link. Frames allow you to supply commentary on material in another site and also to maintain navigation links back to your site (see Chapter 4, *Frames*).

PLACING LINKS

Links are a <u>distraction</u>. It is pointless to <u>write a paragraph</u> and then fill it with <u>invitations</u> to your <u>reader</u> to <u>go elsewhere</u>. You can minimize the disruptive quality of links by managing their placement on the page. Put only the most salient links within the body of your text, and remember that these links should open new browser windows so that you don't supplant the original pages. But most links do not belong in the middle of the page—they won't be important enough to justify the potential distractions they pose.

Group all minor, illustrative, parenthetic, or footnote links at the bottom of the document where they are available but not distracting.

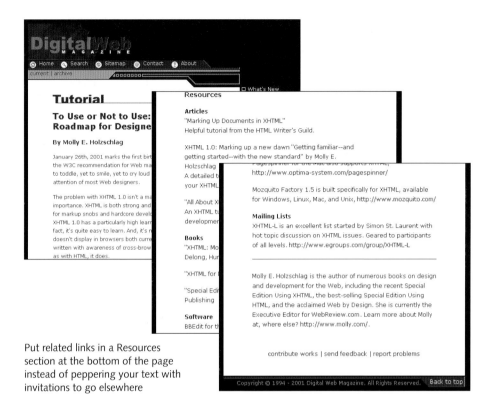

Put related links in a Resources section at the bottom of the page instead of peppering your text with invitations to go elsewhere

If you do place links in the body of your text, pay close attention to your language. Never construct a sentence around a link phrase, such as "click here for more information." Write the sentence as you normally would, and place the link anchor on the word or words that best describe the additional content you are linking to.

- Poor: <u>Click here</u> for more information on placing links within your text.
- Better: Avoid problems with Web links by <u>managing their placement</u> within the context of your document.

REFERENCES

Associated Press. 2000. *The Associated Press stylebook and briefing on media law*. Cambridge, Mass.: Perseus.

Hale, Constance, and Jessie Scanlon. 1999. *Wired style: Principles of English usage in the digital age*. New York: Broadway Books.

Krug, Steve. 2001. *Don't make me think! A common sense approach to Web usability.* Indianapolis, Ind.: Que.

Microsoft Corporation. 1995. *The Microsoft manual of style for technical publications.* Redmond, Wash.: Microsoft Press.

Mullen, R. 1998. *The HTML 4 programmer's reference: All platforms.* Research Triangle Park, N.C.: Ventana Press.

New York Times. 1999. *The New York Times manual of style and usage.* New York: Times Books.

Nielsen, Jakob. 1995. *The alertbox: Current issues in Web usability.* http://www.useit.com/alertbox.

———. 1999. *Designing Web usability: The practice of simplicity.* Indianapolis, Ind.: New Riders.

Strunk, Jr., William, and E. B. White. 2000. *The elements of style,* 4th ed. New York: Macmillan.

Zinsser, William. 1998. *On writing well: An informal guide to writing nonfiction.* 6th ed. New York: HarperReference.

7   *Web Graphics*

We know that the tail must wag the dog,
for the horse is drawn by the cart;
But the Devil whoops, as he whooped of old:
"It's clever, but is it Art?"
—Rudyard Kipling, "The Conundrum of the Workshops"

IN THIS CHAPTER we show you techniques to optimize the look and efficiency of your Web page graphics. Although electronic publishing frees you from the cost and limitations of color reproduction on paper, you will still need to make careful calculations (and a few compromises) if you wish to optimize your graphics and photographs for various display monitors and Internet access speeds.

CHARACTERISTICS OF WEB GRAPHICS

The parameters that influence the display of Web graphics are the user's display monitor and bandwidth capacity. A good segment of the Web audience accesses the Internet via modem, and many view Web pages on monitors that display only 256 colors. This reality imposes limits on the size of files and number of colors that can be included in Web graphics.

COLOR DISPLAYS

Color monitors for desktop microcomputers are based on cathode ray tubes (CRTs) or back-lighted flat-screen technologies. Because monitors transmit light, displays use the red-green-blue (RGB) additive color model. The RGB model is called "additive" because a combination of the three pure colors red, green, and blue "adds up" to white light:

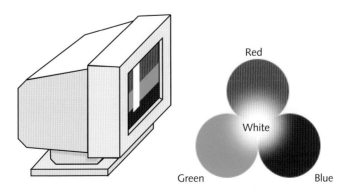

The computer's operating system organizes the display screen into a grid of *x* and *y* coordinates, like a checkerboard. Each little box on the screen is called a "pixel" (short for "picture element"). Current Macintosh and Windows displays are composed of these grids of pixels.

Pixels and color depth   To control the color of each pixel on the screen, the operating system must dedicate a small amount of memory to each pixel. In aggregate this memory dedicated to the display screen is often referred to as "video RAM" or "VRAM" (Video Random Access Memory). In the simplest form of black-and-white computer displays, a single bit of memory is assigned to each pixel. Because each memory bit is either positive or negative (0 or 1), a 1-bit display system can manage only two colors (black or white) for each pixel on the screen:

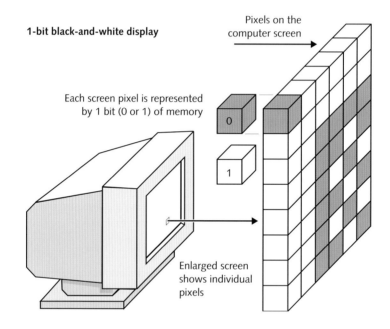

1-bit black-and-white display

Pixels on the computer screen

Each screen pixel is represented by 1 bit (0 or 1) of memory

0

1

Enlarged screen shows individual pixels

If more bits of memory are dedicated to each pixel in the display, more colors can be managed. When 8 bits of memory are dedicated to each pixel, each pixel could be one of 256 colors. (256 = 2 to the eighth power; in other words, 256 is the maximum number of unique combinations of zeros and ones you can make with 8 bits.) This kind of computer display is called an "8-bit" or "256-color" display, and is common on older laptop computers and desktop machines. Although the exact colors that an 8-bit screen can display are not fixed, there can never be more than 256 unique colors on the screen at once:

8-bit, or 256-color display

Each screen pixel is represented
by 8 bits of memory

256 colors (Color palette, or color lookup table)

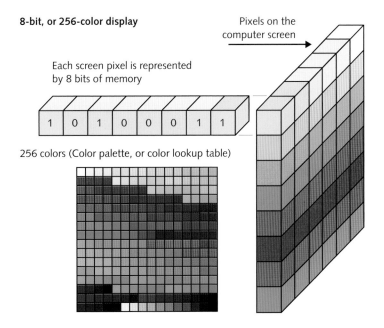

Pixels on the
computer screen →

If still more memory is dedicated to each pixel, nearly photographic color is achievable on the computer screen. "True-color" or "24-bit" color displays can show millions of unique colors simultaneously on the computer screen. True-color images are composed by dedicating 24 bits of memory to each pixel; 8 each for the red, green, and blue components (8 + 8 + 8 = 24):

24-bit "true color" display

Each screen pixel is represented by three groups
of 8 pixels, for a total of 24 bits

Red   Green   Blue

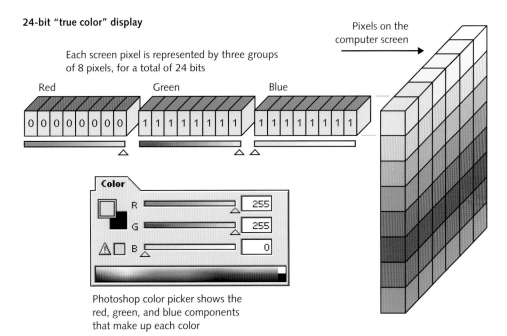

Pixels on the
computer screen →

Photoshop color picker shows the
red, green, and blue components
that make up each color

The amount of VRAM dedicated to each screen pixel in the display is commonly referred to as the "color depth" of the monitor. Most Macintosh and Windows microcomputers sold in recent years can easily display color depths in thousands (16-bit) or millions (24-bit) of simultaneous colors. To check your computer system for the range of color depths available to you, use the "Display" control panel (Windows) or the "Monitors" control panel (Macintosh):

Windows   **Macintosh**

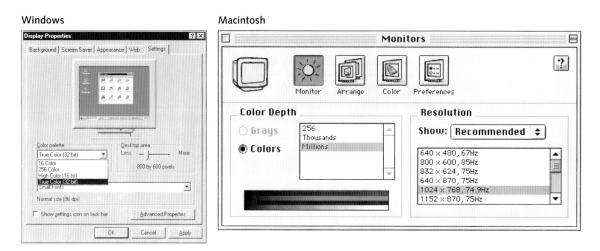

Color depth and graphics files   The terminology and memory schemes used in color displays are directly analogous to those used to describe color depth in graphics files. In their uncompressed states, 8-bit, or 256-color, image files dedicate 8 bits to each color pixel in the image. In 8-bit images the 256 colors that make up the image are stored in an array called a "palette" or an "index." The color palette may also be referred to as a "color lookup table" (CLUT). As mentioned above, 8-bit images can never contain more than 256 unique colors:

256-color
palette

True-color, or 24-bit, images are typically much larger than 8-bit images in their uncompressed state, because 24 bits of memory are dedicated to each pixel, typically arranged in three monochrome layers—red, green, and blue:

Red layer (8 bits)

Green layer (8 bits)

Blue layer (8 bits)

Composite RGB image

The color management system currently used by Web browser software is based on an 8-bit, 216-color (not 256) palette. The browser-safe color palette is a solution devised by Netscape to solve the problem of displaying color graphics in a similar way on many kinds of display screens, with browsers running under different operating systems (such as Macintosh, Windows, and UNIX). Because a majority of the Web audience years ago had 8-bit display screens, 256 colors was the upper limit for the color palette. But the various versions of the Windows operating system (which currently represent about 95 percent of the microcomputer market) reserve 40 colors for displaying such graphic interface elements as windows, menus, screen wallpaper, icons, and buttons, which leaves just 216 colors to display everything else. The 216 colors chosen by Netscape are identical in both the Macintosh and Windows system palettes. Although the browser-safe color scheme originated at Netscape, at present both of the dominant Web browsers (Netscape Navigator and Microsoft Internet Explorer) use the same color management system.

Most Web users have computers and monitors set to "thousands" or "millions" of colors, so the importance of the so-called Web-safe palette has sharply diminished in the past few years. When the user has a monitor set to thousands or millions of colors *all* colors display properly, so there is no longer any need to restrict your color choices to the 216 Web-safe colors.

Windows
256 colors

Macintosh
256 colors

Browser-safe palette
216 colors

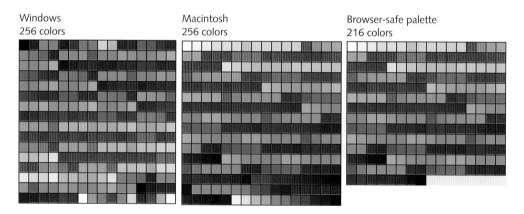

Full-color photographs may contain an almost infinite range of color values. Dithering is the most common means of reducing the color range of images down to the 256 (or fewer) colors seen in 8-bit GIF images.

Dithering is the process of juxtaposing pixels of two colors to create the illusion that a third color is present. A simple example is an image with only black and white in the color palette. By combining black and white pixels in complex patterns a graphics program like Adobe Photoshop can create the illusion of gray values:

Full-color image
dithered
to two colors

The same process softens the effect of reducing the number of colors in full-color images:

Original full-color photograph

Dithered to 256 colors

Most images are dithered in a diffusion or randomized pattern to diminish the harsh transition from one color to another. But dithering also reduces the overall sharpness of an image, and it often introduces a noticeable grainy pattern in the image. This loss of image detail is especially apparent when full-color photos are dithered down to the 216-color browser-safe palette:

Original full-tone image

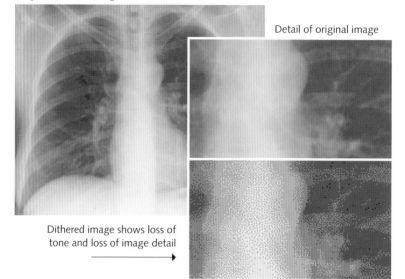

Detail of original image

Dithered image shows loss of
tone and loss of image detail
———————————————▶

Dithering done by the browser   If a reader of your Web site has his or her display monitor set to 256 colors (an increasingly rare occurrence these days), then the Web browser will display images using the 216-color browser-safe color palette. In this situation there is no way to force the browser to display a color outside the browser-safe palette. If any of your photographs, graphic design elements, or background colors use hues outside the browser-safe palette, the Web browser will automatically dither the displayed images into the browser-safe colors. The effect of using "unsafe" colors for your major graphic elements is that readers with 256-color displays will see a lot of heavily dithered images. This may be acceptable for some visual elements on the page, but if your basic navigation buttons and background graphics are dithered, parts of the page will be hard to read and the overall effect will be amateurish:

Navigation graphics done in   Graphics not done in browser-safe
browser-safe colors   colors dither on 256-color screens

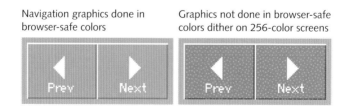

Coping with browser-safe colors   Now that the vast majority of Web users have more sophisticated display screens most designers choose to use GIF graphics with custom colors or full-color JPEG graphics and just accept that they will dither on some small percentage of display screens that are still set to 256 colors. One compromise is to mix navigation graphics done in browser-safe colors with full-color JPEG graphics. The full-color images will be dithered on 256-color screens, but the navigation buttons will look the same on all screens.

GIF graphics, in browser colors

JPEG graphics, full-color

GIF graphics, in browser colors

Screen resolution refers to the number of pixels a screen can display within a given area. Screen resolution is usually expressed in pixels per linear inch of screen. Most personal computer displays have resolutions that vary from 72 to 96 pixels per inch (ppi). The resolution of the display screen is dependent on how the monitor and display card are configured, but it's safe to assume that most users fall into the lower end of the range, or about 72 to 80 ppi.

Images destined for print can be created at various resolutions, but images for Web pages are always limited by the resolution of the computer screen. Thus a square GIF graphic of 72 by 72 pixels will be approximately one inch square on a 72-ppi display monitor. When you are creating graphics for Web pages you should always use the 1:1 display ratio (one pixel in the image equals one pixel on the screen), because this is how big the image will display on the Web page. Images that are too large should be reduced in size with a sophisticated image editor like Adobe's Photoshop to display at proper size at a resolution of 72 ppi.

GAMMA

In computer imaging and display screens "gamma" refers to the degree of contrast between the midlevel gray values of an image. The technical explanations of gamma are irrelevant here—the visual effect of changing gamma values is easy to see. If you own a copy of Adobe ImageReady, open an image with an average range of colors and contrasts and use the "Image: Adjust: Gamma" control to change the gamma settings (see the Image-Ready manual for details). Images will change noticeably with even minor changes in gamma settings. Gamma considerations are particularly important if you are displaying images with very long gray scales (such as medical diagnostic images and fine black-and-white photography) or images in which the exact color values are critical (such as works of art and clinical medical photographs):

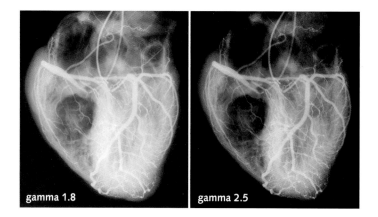

The default gamma settings for Macintosh (1.8 target gamma) and Windows (2.2 target gamma) monitors are quite different, and this can lead to unpleasant surprises when you first see your images displayed on "the other" platform. Mac users will see darker and more contrasting images on Windows displays; Windows users will see flat and washed-out images on Mac displays. Most Web designers opt for a middle-ground solution, lightening images slightly if they work on the Macintosh; darkening slightly and adding a little contrast if they work in Windows.

GRAPHICS AND NETWORK BANDWIDTH

Many Web users currently access their Internet service providers via 56 kilobits per second (KBPS) modems from their homes, offices, or remote work sites. At 56 KBPS the actual download rate is only about 7 kilobytes (KB) per second (8 bits make a byte). This means that a modest 36 KB graphic on your Web page could take five seconds or longer to load into the reader's Web browser. Actual data transmission rates will vary depending on the user's modem, Web server speed, Internet connection, and other factors, but the overall point is clear: the more graphics you incorporate, the longer the reader will have to wait to see your page. A full-screen graphic menu on your home page plus background graphics could leave your modem-based readers twiddling their thumbs for a full minute or more, even if they have a state-of-the-art modem and a good Internet connection. Look at your watch (better yet, hold your breath) for a full minute, then decide whether you're willing to ask your users to wait this long when they visit your Web site.

A better strategy is to increase the graphics loading of your pages gradually, drawing users into your site with reasonable download times. As readers become more engaged with your content, they will be more willing to endure longer delays, especially if you give them notes about the size of graphics or warnings that particular pages are full of graphics and will take longer to download. At today's average modem speeds most pages designed for users dialing in from home should contain no more than 50 to 75 kilobytes of graphics.

Graphics and intranets   Luckily for graphic designers, many Web sites are created primarily for educational, organizational, and commercial users who access their local intranets and the larger World Wide Web from the school or office at Ethernet speeds or greater. Also, increasing numbers of home users now have access to higher-speed connections like DSL and cable modems. Graphics and page performance are also an issue for these users, but it makes little sense to restrict Web page graphics arbitrarily in the cause of "saving network bandwidth." The bandwidth gearheads always miss the point: graphics are what drew most people to the Web in the first place. If you've got the access speed, indulge!

GRAPHIC FILE FORMATS

Because of the bandwidth issues surrounding networked delivery of information and because image files contain so much information, Web graphics are by necessity compressed. Different graphic file formats employ varying compression schemes, and some are designed to work better than others for certain types of graphics. The two primary Web file formats are GIF and JPEG. A third format, PNG, has been available since 1995 but has been little used because of poor browser support.

GIF FILES

The CompuServe Information Service popularized the Graphic Interchange Format in the 1980s as an efficient means to transmit images across data networks. In the early 1990s the original designers of the World Wide Web adopted GIF for its efficiency and widespread familiarity. The overwhelming majority of images on the Web are now in GIF format, and virtually all Web browsers that support graphics can display GIF files. GIF files incorporate a compression scheme to keep file sizes at a minimum, and they are limited to 8-bit (256 or fewer colors) color palettes. Several slight variants of the basic GIF format add support for transparent color and for the interlaced GIF graphics popularized by Netscape Navigator.

GIF *file compression*   The GIF file format uses a relatively basic form of file compression (Lempel Zev Welch, or LZW) that squeezes out inefficiencies in the data storage without losing data or distorting the image. The LZW compression scheme is best at compressing images with large fields of homogeneous color. It is less efficient at compressing complicated pictures with many colors and complex textures:

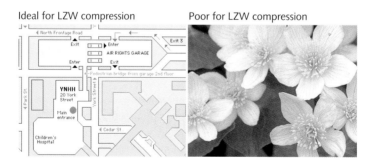

Ideal for LZW compression   Poor for LZW compression

Improving GIF *compression*   You can take advantage of the characteristics of LZW compression to improve its efficiency and thereby reduce the size of your GIF graphics. The strategy is to reduce the number of colors in your GIF image to the minimum number necessary and to remove stray colors that are not required to represent the image. A GIF graphic cannot have more than 256 colors but it can have fewer colors, down to the minimum of two (black and white). Images with fewer colors will compress more efficiently under LZW compression.

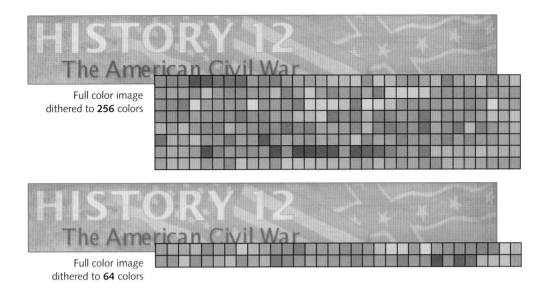

Full color image
dithered to **256** colors

Full color image
dithered to **64** colors

Interlaced GIF   The conventional (non-interlaced) GIF graphic downloads one line of pixels at a time from top to bottom, and browsers display each line of the image as it gradually builds on the screen. In interlaced GIF files the image data is stored in a format that allows browsers that support interlaced GIFs to begin to build a low-resolution version of the full-sized GIF picture on the screen while the file is downloading. Many people find the "fuzzy-to-sharp" animated effect of interlacing visually appealing, but the most important benefit of interlacing is that it gives the reader a preview of the full area of the picture while the picture downloads into the browser.

Interlacing is best for larger GIF images such as illustrations and photographs. Interlacing is a poor choice for small GIF graphics such as navigation bars, buttons, and icons. These small graphics will load onto the screen much faster if you keep them in conventional (non-interlaced) GIF format. In general, interlacing has no significant effect on the file size of GIF graphics.

Half of figure downloaded,
non-interlaced GIF

Half of figure downloaded,
interlaced GIF

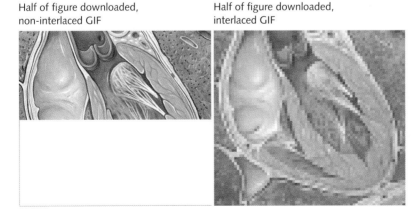

Transparent GIF   The GIF format allows you to pick colors from the color lookup table of the GIF to be transparent. You can use image-editing software like Photoshop (and many shareware utility programs) to select colors in a GIF graphic's color palette to become transparent. Usually the color selected for transparency is the background color in the graphic.

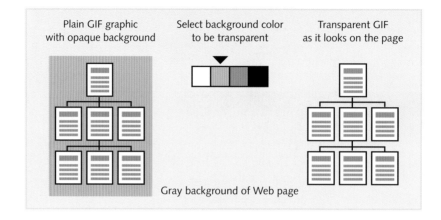

Unfortunately, the transparent property is not selective; if you make a color transparent, every pixel in the graphic that shares that particular color will become also transparent. This can cause unexpected results:

Plain GIF graphic with opaque background color

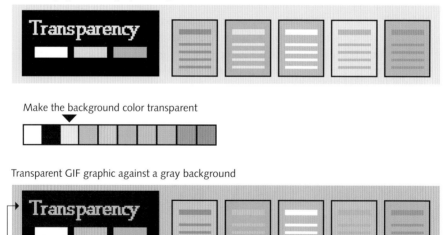

All pixels of the transparent color disappear, not just the background

Adding transparency to a GIF graphic can produce disappointing results when the image contains antialiasing (see Chapter 5, *Antialiased type*). If you use an image-editing program like Photoshop to create a shape set against a background color, Photoshop will smooth the shape by inserting pixels of intermediate colors along the shape's boundary edges. This smoothing, or *antialiasing*, improves the look of screen images by softening jagged edges. Trouble starts when you set the background color to transparent and then use the image on a Web page against a different background color. The antialiased pixels in the image will still correspond to the original background color. In the example below, when we change the background color from white to transparent (letting the gray Web page background show through), an ugly white halo appears around the graphic:

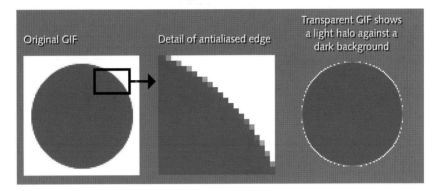

Transparency works best with simple diagrammatic graphics, but it can also work with complex shapes. The GIF graphic of the watercolor painting below (from the second edition of the online version of this guide) can run across the scan column and into the white background because we made the white background of the sparrow painting transparent. We avoided potential problems with a light halo around the leaves in the gray scan column area by retouching the painting to remove the white antialiased "halo" from the leaf edges:

Animated GIF   The GIF file format allows you to combine multiple GIF images into a single file to create animation. There are a number of drawbacks to this functionality, however. The GIF format applies no compression between frames, so if you are combining four 30-kilobyte images into a single animation, you will end up with a 120 KB GIF file to push through the wire. The load is lightened somewhat by the fact that animated GIF files stream to the user, so the frames load and play even before the entire file is downloaded. Another drawback of GIF animations is that they are an imposition and a potential distraction. Because there are no interface controls for this file format, GIF animations play whether you want them to or not. And if looping is enabled, the animations play again and again and again. GIF animations are rarely used in a meaningful way, and generally distract readers from the main content of the page. If you are using GIF animation as content—to illustrate a concept or technique where animation is really required—use the technique sparingly.

The other graphic file format commonly used on the Web to minimize graphics file sizes is the Joint Photographic Experts Group (JPEG) compression scheme. Unlike GIF graphics, JPEG images are full-color images (24 bit, or "true color"). JPEG images have generated tremendous interest among photographers, artists, graphic designers, medical imaging specialists, art historians, and other groups for whom image quality is paramount and where color fidelity cannot be compromised by dithering a graphic to 8-bit color. A newer form of JPEG file called "progressive JPEG" gives JPEG graphics the same gradually built display seen in interlaced GIFs. Like interlaced GIFs, progressive JPEG images often take longer to load onto the page than standard JPEGs, but they do offer the reader a quicker preview.

JPEG compression uses a sophisticated mathematical technique called a discrete cosine transformation to produce a sliding scale of graphics compression. You can choose the degree of compression you wish to apply to an image in JPEG format, but in doing so you also determine the image's quality. The more you squeeze a picture with JPEG compression, the more you degrade its quality. JPEG can achieve incredible compression ratios, squeezing graphics down to as much as one hundred times smaller than the original file. This is possible because the JPEG algorithm discards "unnecessary" data as it compresses the image, and it is thus called a "lossy" compression technique. Notice in the example below how increasing the JPEG compression progressively degrades the details of the image:

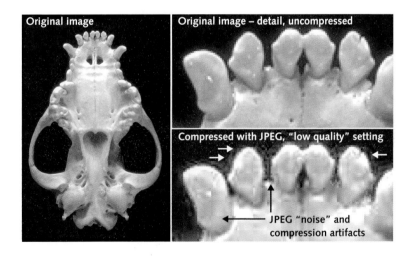

The checkered pattern and the dark "noise" pixels in the compressed image are classic JPEG compression artifacts.

Another example of JPEG compression is shown below. Note the extensive compression noise and distortion present in the bottom dolphin—the download time saved is not worth the degrading of the images.

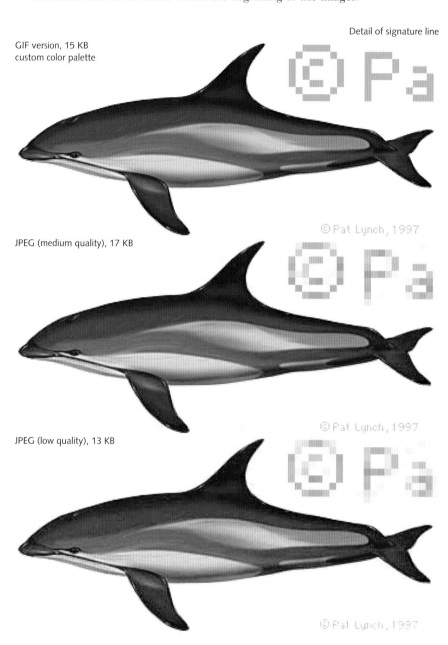

Detail of signature line

GIF version, 15 KB
custom color palette

JPEG (medium quality), 17 KB

JPEG (low quality), 13 KB

Save your original uncompressed images!   Once an image is compressed using JPEG compression, data is lost and you cannot recover it from that image file. Always save an uncompressed original file of your graphics or photographs as backup.

JPEG *image artifacts*   The JPEG algorithm was optimized for compressing conventional pictorial photographs and is also good at handling complex illustrations. Photos and artwork with smooth color and tonal transitions and with few areas of harsh contrast or sharp edges are ideal for JPEG compression. Yet most page design elements, diagrams, typography within images, and many illustrations are composed of hard-edged graphics and bright color boundaries that are seldom encountered in photographs. The illustration below shows what happens when you compress an interface graphic (shown in *a*) in GIF format (*b*, no compression artifacts) and JPEG compression (*c*, with JPEG compression "noise" around the text and borders):

When compressed with JPEG, diagrammatic images such as interface graphics show a noise pattern of compression artifacts around the edges of shapes and text (*c*, above). The JPEG algorithm is best at compressing smooth tonal transitions and cannot properly reproduce the harsh transitions at the edges of diagrammatic graphics.

Portable Network Graphic (PNG, pronounced "ping") is an image format developed by a consortium of graphic software developers as a nonpropri-etary alternative to the GIF image format. As mentioned earlier, Com-puServe developed the GIF format, and GIF uses the proprietary LZW com-pression scheme owned by Unisys Corporation. Any graphics tool developer who makes software that saves in GIF format must pay a royalty to Unisys and CompuServe.

PNG graphics were designed specifically for use on Web pages, and they offer a range of attractive features that should eventually make PNG the most common graphic format. These features include a full range of color depths, support for sophisticated image transparency, better interlacing, and automatic corrections for display monitor gamma. PNG images can also hold a short text description of the image's content, which allows Internet search engines to search for images based on these embedded text descriptions. Un-fortunately, the PNG graphic format is not yet widely supported, and the cur-rent implementation of PNG graphics in the major Web browsers does not fully support all of PNG's features. This should change over the next few years, but do not make a commitment to PNG graphics until you are sure that most of your audience is using browsers that support PNG.

IMAGING STRATEGIES

Interface elements　Small page navigation graphics, buttons, and graphic de-sign elements should be handled as non-interlaced GIF graphics. The most conservative approach would be to use colors from the 216-color browser ("Web safe") palette so that they never dither, even on 8-bit display screens. Or, if you choose to use a color scheme for your interface that is not restricted to the Web palette, check to see that the colors you choose default to accept-able alternatives on 8-bit displays.

Photographs as GIFs　When you convert a full-color image into an 8-bit (256-color) GIF file you could allow Photoshop to choose the 256 colors that best fit that particular image. This results in the optimal GIF image quality—often these images look almost as good as their full-color origi-nals—but the creation of a custom color palette does have drawbacks. If the reader of your page has their monitor set to show only 256 colors at one time then the colors in your GIF images will appear distorted as the browser forces them to display using the 216-color browser palette. Forcing a GIF made from custom palette colors to display within the limited system palette colors can result in ugly distortions of the image. A Web browser running on an 8-bit display has no way to optimize your particular custom GIF colors—it forces the picture to display in the nearest equivalent colors in the browser palette. The result is often color banding, or harsh distortions of the original colors, as seen in the example below:

To get around this problem you could convert all your color graphics to GIF files that use only the browser palette of 216 colors. This would ensure that your images look exactly the same—in most cases, poor—no matter how the user's display screen is set up. A better approach is to apply custom palettes to your images and accept that those readers using 8-bit display monitors (a growing minority) will see distorted images. Or you could use the JPEG file format instead.

The image compression in the GIF file format is less efficient than JPEG compression. However, the compression advantages of JPEG don't apply to small to medium-size images (say, up to 200 × 200 pixels). At these sizes GIF images may be only slightly larger than JPEG files. With images larger than 200 × 200 the compression advantages of the JPEG format become more obvious.

Photographs as JPEGS JPEG files are inherently full-color (24-bit) images, so preserving the correct colors in the files themselves is not an issue. However, there is no way to prevent JPEG images from dithering when they are displayed on 8-bit screens—any photographic image displayed on a 256-color display will dither. The dithering seen in JPEG images does not compromise image quality any more than if you dithered the images to 256-color GIFs yourself. If you standardize on JPEG images, the majority of your audience will see full-color photographs and illustrations. Standardize on the JPEG format for any photographic or other full-color or grayscale image suitable for JPEG compression.

Diagrams and illustrations as vector graphics Most Web page graphics are raster images—often called "bitmap" or "paint" images—composed of a grid of colored pixels. Complex diagrams or illustrations, however, should be created as vector graphics and then converted to raster formats like GIF or JPEG for the Web. Vector graphics (also known as "draw" or "PostScript" graphics) are composed of mathematical descriptions of lines and shapes. Although these graphics cannot (yet) be used directly to illustrate Web pages without requiring users to have a special browser plug-in, there are three major reasons for producing complex diagrams in vector graphics programs:

1 Vector graphic illustrations are automatically antialiased when imported into Photoshop or other raster imaging programs and converted to raster graphics:

Illustrator artwork, imported but not antialiased

Same graphic, antialiased on import into Photoshop

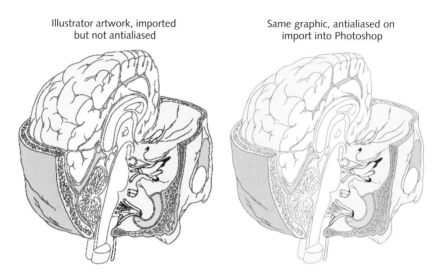

2 Vector graphics can be easily resized as they are imported:

Three Photoshop renderings from the same PostScript vector drawing, antialiased

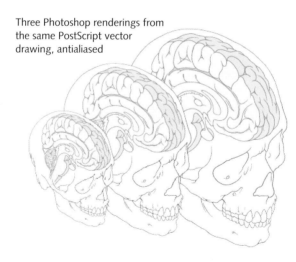

3 Complex artwork created in such vector-based programs as Adobe Illustrator and Macromedia FreeHand is a better investment of your illustration budget, because vector graphics also produce high-resolution images suitable for print, as shown below. The illustrations below and immediately above were produced from the same Illustrator file:

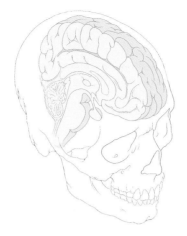

Archiving your Web site graphics   Always save a copy of your original graphics files, and make it a standard practice to create separate new files every time you make significant changes to an image, such as resizing it or changing the file format. After the close of a project all photos and artwork should be kept and stored at their full original resolution and in a format that does not compromise the image quality of the files through "lossy" image compression, as in JPEG. We prefer to archive every image generated in a project. Many small 8-bit GIF or JPEG illustrations on the finished Web page, for example, start out as much larger high-resolution files in Photoshop format. We save all the intermediate pieces, not just the original and final files. This will save you a lot of time if you later change your mind about the best file format for a graphic or need to modify it. If you have archived the full-color Photoshop version of the graphic, you can easily create a new version in a different format. If you save only the final GIFs, you will have lost your full-color version. If you save only the final JPEGs, you will no longer have images without compression artifacts, and recompressing an image that already has JPEG compression noise usually yields poor results.

SUMMARY-FILE FORMATS

Uses for GIF *and* JPEG *Files*   Netscape Navigator, Microsoft Internet Explorer, and most other browsers support both GIF and JPEG graphics (as of this writing, PNG graphics are not adequately supported). In theory, you could use either graphic format for the visual elements of your Web pages. In practice, however, most Web developers will continue to favor the GIF format for most page design elements, diagrams, and images that must not dither on 8-bit display screens. Designers choose the JPEG format mostly for photographs, complex "photographic" illustrations, medical images, and other types of images in which the compression artifacts of the JPEG process do not severely compromise image quality.

Advantages of GIF *files*

- GIF is the most widely supported graphics format on the Web
- GIFs of diagrammatic images look better than JPEGS
- GIF supports transparency and interlacing

Advantages of JPEG *images*

- Huge compression ratios mean faster download speeds
- JPEG produces excellent results for most photographs and complex images
- JPEG supports full-color (24-bit, "true color") images

IMAGES ON THE SCREEN

The primary challenge in creating images for Web pages is the relatively low resolution of the computer screen. But today's computer screens can display thousands or millions of colors, and this wealth of color minimizes the limitations of screen resolution. Complex graphics or color photographs often look surprisingly good on Web pages for two reasons:

- True-color (24-bit) or high-color (16-bit) displays show enough colors to reproduce photographs and complex art accurately
- The light transmitted from display monitors shows more dynamic range and color intensity than light reflected from printed pages

Digital publishing is color publishing: on the Web there is no economic penalty for publishing in color. Web pages may in fact be the best current means of distributing color photography—it's a lot cheaper than color printing, and it's also more consistent and reliable than all but the most expert (and costly) color printing.

THE SCREEN VERSUS PRINTED COLOR ARTWORK

Relative to printed pages the computer screen is a low-resolution medium. When you look at illustrations, photographs, and other sophisticated imagery, however, the differences in quality between conventional four-color printing and the computer screen are not as great as you might expect.

In terms of resolution, the computer screen is limited to about 72 to 92 dots per inch of resolution (see *Screen resolution*, above). But most four-color magazine printing is done at 150 dpi, or only about four times the resolution of the computer screen (150 dpi is four times the resolution of 75 dpi because resolution is measured over area, 150 × 150 per square inch):

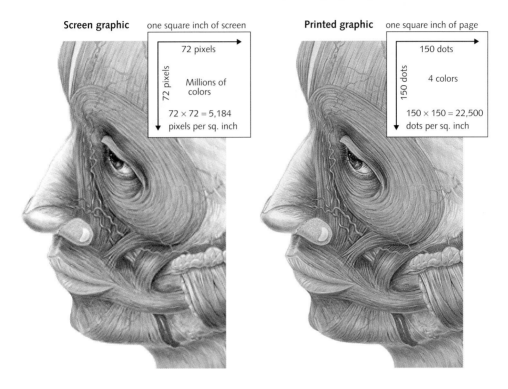

Screen graphic — one square inch of screen

72 pixels
72 pixels
Millions of colors
72 × 72 = 5,184 pixels per sq. inch

Printed graphic — one square inch of page

150 dots
150 dots
4 colors
150 × 150 = 22,500 dots per sq. inch

Regarding color reproduction, four-color printed images are separated into four subtractive printing colors (cyan, magenta, yellow, and black). These four inks combined produce the illusion of a full range of colors on the printed page, but ultimately the typical magazine or textbook image is composed of only four colors. By comparison, as mentioned, current computer monitors can display millions of colors, producing a richness of color that easily rivals the best quality color printing. Also, computer screens display transilluminated images—the colored light shines out from the screen. Transilluminated images deliver a much greater range of contrast and color intensity than images printed on opaque paper, which depend on reflected light. Finally, computer displays show color images using the additive RGB (red-green-blue) color system, which can display a much broader and subtler range of colors than conventional four-color printing.

Bottom line: the computer screen is lower in resolution, but because of the other advantages of computer displays, images on Web pages can easily rival color images printed on paper.

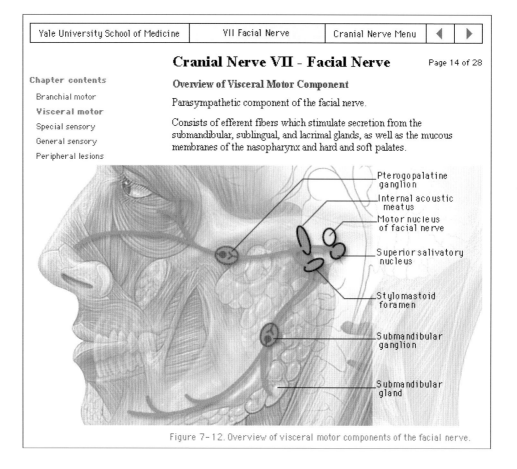

Cranial Nerve VII – Facial Nerve

Chapter contents

Branchial motor

Visceral motor

Special sensory

General sensory

Peripheral lesions

Overview of Visceral Motor Component

Parasympathetic component of the facial nerve.

Consists of efferent fibers which stimulate secretion from the submandibular, sublingual, and lacrimal glands, as well as the mucous membranes of the nasopharynx and hard and soft palates.

Pterogopalatine ganglion

Internal acoustic meatus

Motor nucleus of facial nerve

Superior salivatory nucleus

Stylomastoid foramen

Submandibular ganglion

Submandibular gland

Figure 7–12. Overview of visceral motor components of the facial nerve.

COMPLEX ILLUSTRATIONS OR PHOTOGRAPHS

The anatomic graphic above was originally painted at much higher resolution in Adobe Photoshop (1000 × 2000 pixels, 24-bit RGB file). We then reduced a copy to the size above and used Photoshop's "Unsharp Mask" filter (at 60 percent) to restore sharpness. Although this small version of the painting has lost some resolution and color detail, it still shows all the major anatomic landmarks. The extra detail and subtle nuances of high-resolution artwork are not entirely lost when the graphic is reduced to Web page size. We chose the JPEG file format for the anatomic painting because the artwork is relatively large for a Web page graphic. JPEG compression can be used for paintings or photographs with text labels if you choose the right compression setting. The painting above was compressed in Photoshop at "good" quality, which is the medium-quality setting ("excellent, good, poor"). If you choose the "good" or "excellent" JPEG compression settings, text labels should look acceptable, at least on 16-bit or 24-bit displays. Note that in the anatomic illustration example shown above the text labels are clear and legible, even though close inspection would certainly turn up JPEG noise around the characters.

Basic diagrams also work well on the computer screen if they are carefully designed to match the grid of pixels on the screen. Graphics built with orthogonal lines (straight horizontal or vertical lines) or diagonal lines at 45-degree angles work best for the screen, as this enlarged view illustrates:

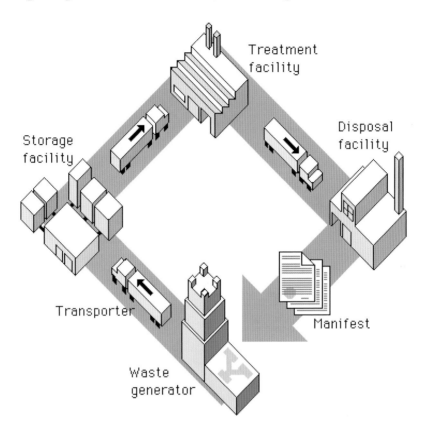

Complex icons are hard to interpret, and they look mushy and confusing on the screen. Keep icons and navigation graphics as simple as possible:

Simple isometric perspective graphics also work well because they depend on straight lines and 45-degree diagonals. Although the restrictions of working within fixed line angles make the technique unsuitable for many diagrammatic graphics, it is possible to build complex illustrations using this technique. The regularity of the isometric line work and the absence of the complexities of perspective bring order to graphics that might otherwise be too complex for Web page presentation:

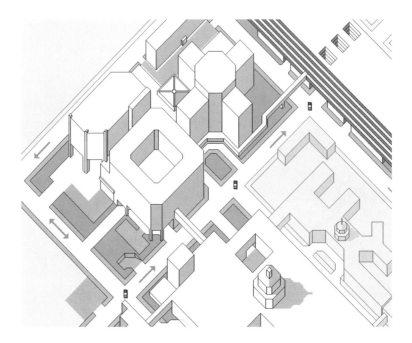

Another benefit of keeping diagrammatic art and maps simple is that graphic simplicity is ideally suited to the LZW encoding compression algorithm used in GIF graphics (see GIF *files*, above). This 828×525-pixel GIF graphic is large for a Web page, but it compresses to a mere 27 KB because the contents are well suited to LZW compression:

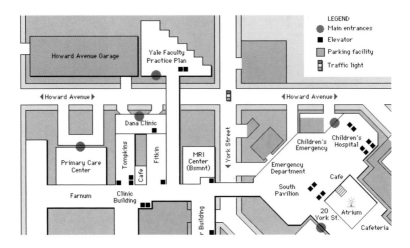

Be careful about choosing the proper sizes for this type of illustration. Graphics carefully built to match the pixel grid cannot be resized automatically in Photoshop—they must be redrawn by hand to larger or smaller sizes to avoid a mushy, fuzzy look that destroys their effectiveness:

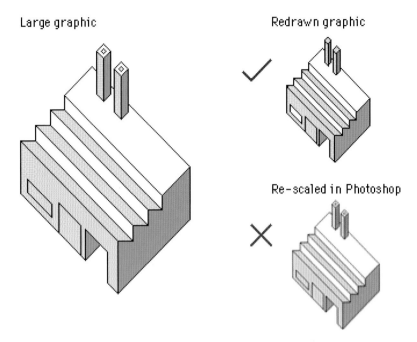

Large graphic

Redrawn graphic

Re-scaled in Photoshop

The low resolution of the computer screen is insufficient for displaying diagrams that incorporate many curves or angles; lines that do not follow the pixel grid appear jagged. To optimize these kinds of diagrams for Web pages you'll need to use antialiasing to smooth the boundaries and make the jagged edges less apparent:

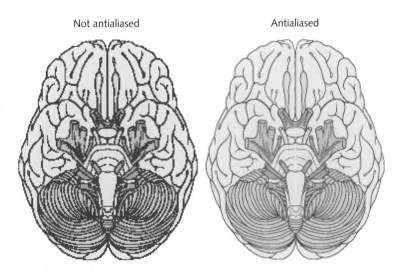

Not antialiased

Antialiased

At great magnification antialiased graphics may have fuzzy boundaries, but at normal magnification antialiasing produces smooth, natural-looking line work.

HTML AND GRAPHICS

Height and width tags   All your page graphics source tags (even small button or icon graphics) should include HEIGHT and WIDTH tags. These tags tell the browser how much space to devote to a graphic on a page, and they instruct the browser to lay out your Web page even before the graphics files have begun to download. Although this does not speed up downloading (only a faster data connection can do that), it does allow the user to see the page layout more quickly. The text blocks will fill out first and then the graphics files will "pour" into the allotted spaces. This means that the user can start to read your page while the graphics are downloading.

Colored backgrounds   Web background colors offer a "zero-bandwidth" means to change the look of your pages without adding graphics. They also allow you to increase the legibility of your pages, tune the background color to complement foreground art, and signal a broad change in context from one part of your site to another. A List Apart uses background colors as an easy way to enliven the visual impact of their otherwise low-bandwidth pages:

A LIST APART — For People Who Make Websites.

Articles on **CSS** below or visit our **CSS Forum**.

Browse issues 1–30, 31–60, 61–90, 91–current or *previous issues*

Select category... | go

No.	Title & Author	Tragically Hip Synopsis
119	Practical CSS Layout Tips, Tricks & Techniques Mark Newhouse	Think you need HTML tables to craft complex liquid layouts? Not so! In this tip-packed tutorial, Mark Newhouse shares advanced yet practical CSS techniques any working web designer can use.
116	CSS Talking Points Greg Kise	Selling your clients on standards-compliant design doesn't have to hurt. Kise's four-point CSS Selling Plan helps the medicine go down.
109	Size Matters Todd Fahrner	CSS includes seven font-size keywords intended to give site designers the power to control the size of type on the page without creating accessibility problems. Unfortunately, keywords fail in most browsers. Fortunately, Todd Fahrner has a workaround.
105	From Web Hacks to Web Standards: A Designer's Journey Zeldman	ALA Issue No. 99, originally published 16 February, helped launch a CSS redesign craze. But the issue's reliance on CSS-2 selectors caused problems in IE6 beta and IE4.5/Mac. So we've redesigned the issue and updated A Web Designer's Journey to include more info, more tips, and more resources.
99	To Hell With Bad Browsers! ALA	Why does ALA look like @#$ in your 4.0 browser? Read this now.
		If you wish to control your web typography, CSS

Picking the background color is easy in WYSIWYG (what you see is what you get) graphic Web page layout programs. Unfortunately, picking a color without one of these Web page editors is a procedure only a propellerhead could enjoy. The color is specified in the tag in hexadecimal code, in which the six elements give the red, green, and blue values that blend to make the color. In the tag, the hex code is always preceded by a "#" sign: (#RRGGBB). Because this whole business is now handled visually by the new generation of WYSIWYG page editors and image editors like Adobe Photoshop, we will not delve further into the arcana of hexadecimal RGB color selection.

Background colors and legibility   The Web is rife with pages whose legibility is marginal due to poorly chosen background color–text color combinations. Text that is hard to read is a hindrance for a fully sighted reader, and certain color combinations make pages unreadable for colorblind users (10 percent of males are partially colorblind). The legibility of type on the computer screen is already compromised by low screen resolution. The typical Macintosh or Windows computer screen displays text at 72 to 80 dots per inch (about 5,200 dots per square inch), or almost 300 times lower resolution than a typical magazine page (1,440,000 dots per square inch). Black text on a white (or very *slightly* tinted) background yields the best overall type contrast and legibility. Black backgrounds are significantly less legible than white backgrounds, even when white type is used for maximum contrast. Colored backgrounds can work as an alternative to plain browser-default gray if the colors are kept in very muted tones, and low in overall color saturation (pastels, light grays, and light earth tones work best).

Background patterns   Early in 1995 Netscape Navigator version 1.1 gave Web page authors the ability to use small tiled GIF or JPEG graphics (or a single large graphic) to form a background pattern behind the Web page. The feature is controversial in Web design discussions, because pages that use large background images take longer to download and because the background patterns tend to make pages harder to read unless they are carefully designed.

To be suitable for use as a background texture, the graphic should be a small GIF or JPEG, ideally no more than about 100 × 100 pixels in size. In our experience, JPEG background patterns load slightly faster than equivalent GIF graphics. Typical graphics used for background patterns are homogeneous textures:

The image will repeat both horizontally and vertically to fill the browser window.

How you might use background graphics depends entirely on your goals for your Web site, the access speeds that are typical for your target audience, and whether a graphic background matches the aesthetic goals of your Web site. It is foolish to use large or visually complex background textures on any page that is heavily accessed by busy people looking for work-related information—the long download times, amateurish aesthetics, and poor legibility will simply annoy your users. That said, in the hands of a skilled graphic designer who is creating Web pages designed for graphic impact, the option to use background textures opens up many interesting visual design possibilities. This is particularly true in universities and commercial organizations where fast network access is commonplace and bandwidth is not the obstacle it is to many modem-based users.

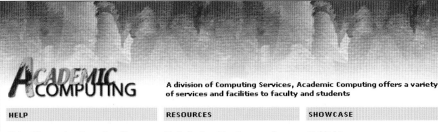

A division of Computing Services, Academic Computing offers a variety of services and facilities to faculty and students

HELP

Help with your hardware & software
Consulting on purchasing decisions, as well as troubleshooting and general computing assistance for academic departments

Using technology in your teaching & research
Services, in-depth support, and help using technology in the classroom

Developing your technology skills
Course offerings, online instruction, and the Faculty Web User Group

Computing Technology Venture Fund
Explorations in applying computing technology in the curriculum

RESOURCES

Tools for teaching & research
Programs and online resources to help you conduct research and deliver your curriculum

Computing facilities
Resources ranging from compute servers and instructional centers to the new Berry Faculty Center

Funding for curricular development
Curricular funding through the Venture Fund and help soliciting grants from external agencies

Student resources
Help for students using computing to fulfill course assignments

SHOWCASE

Highlights
New and noteworthy projects from research and curricular computing

Faculty portfolio
A collection of research and curricular projects illustrating diverse uses of computing

ACADEMIC COMPUTING

Mission and organization
Who we are, what we do, and how we're organized

Contact us
Ways to contact Academic Computing

Imagemaps Imagemaps offer a way to define multiple "live" link areas within a graphic on a Web page. Imagemaps have become a standard feature of most professionally designed Web sites because they offer an effective combination of visual appeal and, when used properly, space-efficient functionality. Imagemaps are particularly effective when incorporated into moderately sized "splash" graphics at the top of home pages or into the "signature" graphics or logos that define your pages. For example, Palm uses a space-efficient imagemap menu on its home page. The graphic is more than a menu; it helps define the signature "look" of pages within the Palm Web site:

Home page

Imagemap menu

Internal page

Imagemaps are the only way to incorporate multiple links into a graphic illustration, as in this anatomic example:

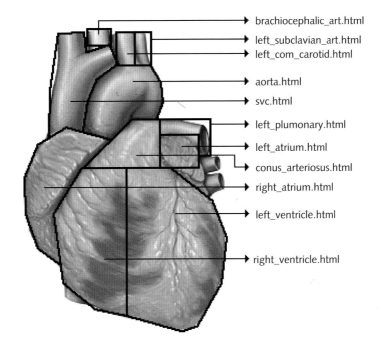

brachiocephalic_art.html
left_subclavian_art.html
left_com_carotid.html

aorta.html

svc.html

left_plumonary.html

left_atrium.html

conus_arteriosus.html

right_atrium.html

left_ventricle.html

right_ventricle.html

Imagemaps are also the ultimate way to overcome the vertical, list-oriented, graphically inflexible norms of conventional Web pages built with standard HTML tags. With imagemaps you can abandon HTML page layout and build links into large graphics, just as you might in CD-ROM authoring programs. Keep in mind, however, that such designs are suitable only for audiences with high bandwidth access to the Web or the local intranet.

ACCESSIBILITY

Whenever you introduce nontext elements to your Web design you reduce the accessibility of your pages. For the purposes of universal access, text is the ultimate content type: it can be most widely adapted for use with different devices and assistive technologies. But the Web is a visual medium, and access to images and other nontext materials is one of the reasons why people turn to the Web over other information sources. As a Web page designer, you should keep this restriction in mind and take measures to ensure that your design decisions do not exclude disabled users from your Web page content.

Text alternates   Your site navigation can be supplied using graphics such as buttons, imagemaps, or animations, but it is *critical* that you design your navigation system for all users. If your site's navigation interface uses graphic menus, always provide an alternate navigation route using basic text links. Users without graphics capabilities, such as those using text-only browsers or visually impaired users, will not be able to use your site if you provide only graphic menus.

ALT-text   HTML has several built-in fallbacks designed to allow your content to degrade gracefully under different viewing conditions. One of these is ALT, an attribute of the IMG tag. The ALT attribute allows you to supply an alternate text description with any images you place on your page. Users who cannot see your images for whatever reason will see or hear the text you supply using the ALT attribute:

```
<IMG SRC="banner.gif" HEIGHT="30" WIDTH="535" ALT="Web Style
Guide">
```

In the above example, users accessing the Web Style Guide page with graphic loading turned off will see the alternate text "Web Style Guide" in place of the banner graphic. Visually impaired users using assistive technology to access Web pages will hear the text "Web Style Guide" read aloud. This way you can use a graphic banner to establish site identity, but users who do not see images will still know what site they are visiting.

eBay users know where they are and can navigate even with images turned off

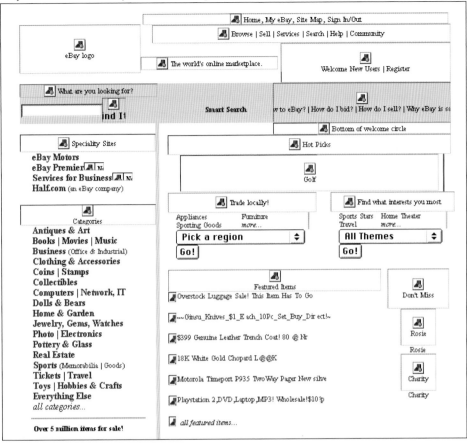

Writing good ALT-text is an epigrammatic art, challenging your ability to describe the content and function of an image in just a few words. Browsers do not currently wrap ALT-text, so users reading ALT-text from the screen will normally see only a few words, though users who are read ALT-text by software will hear the entire description. Think not only about what the image *is* but also how it functions on the page. What does the image say? What is its purpose? Is it there to identify your organization? If so, write ALT-text that identifies your organization. Does it provide navigation options? Write ALT-text that describes where the user will go after clicking on the image. Think about the primary purpose of the graphic and attempt to convey it in ten words or fewer.

```
<IMG SRC="up.gif" HEIGHT="10" WIDTH="10" ALT="Go to top of page">
```

Also include ALT-text describing link destinations for imagemap menus so that users who cannot see the graphic menu will know where they will go if they select an imagemap link.

At times ALT-text is not useful—for example, for interface images like custom bullets or for invisible spacer graphics—and in those cases you should include an empty ALT attribute (ALT="") in your IMG tag. An empty ALT attribute hides the graphic from text-only browsers and assistive technologies like screen readers. If you leave out the ALT-text, users could hear the words "image, image, image, image" because most software is designed to let the user know when there is an undescribed image on the page. If instead you include an empty ALT attribute, the software knows to skip the image.

REFERENCES

Brewer, Judy, ed. 2001. *How people with disabilities use the Web.* http://www.w3c.org/WAI/EO/Drafts/PWD-Use-Web (31 March 2001)

Chisholm, Wendy, Gregg Vanderheiden, and Ian Jacobs, eds. 1999. *Web content accessibility guidelines 1.0.* http://www.w3c.org/TR/WAI-WEBCONTENT/wai-pageauth.html (17 January 2001).

Niederst, Jennifer. 1999. *Web design in a nutshell: A desktop quick reference.* Sebastopol, Calif.: O'Reilly.

Nielsen, Jakob. 1995. *The alertbox: Current issues in Web usability.* http://www.useit.com/alertbox.

———. 1999. *Designing Web usability: The practice of simplicity.* Indianapolis, Ind.: New Riders.

Pring, Robert. 2000. *www.color: Effective use of color in designing Web pages.* New York: Watson-Guptill.

Siegel, David. 1997. *Creating killer Web sites,* 2d ed. Indianapolis, Ind.: Hayden Books.

Webster, Timothy, Paul Atzberger, and Andrew Zolli. 1997. *Web designer's guide to graphics: PNG, GIF, and JPEG.* Indianapolis, Ind.: Hayden Books.

Weinman, Lynda. 1999. *Designing Web graphics: How to prepare images and media for the Web,* 3d ed. Indianapolis, Ind.: New Riders.

8   *Multimedia*

It's as large as life, and twice as natural!
—Lewis Carroll, *Through the Looking-Glass*

PERHAPS THE MOST POWERFUL aspect of computing technology is the ability to combine text, graphics, sounds, and moving images in meaningful ways. The promise of multimedia has been slow to reach the Web because of bandwidth limitations, but each day brings new solutions. Although there are numerous methods for creating Web multimedia, we recommend using stable technology that works for the great majority of client machines. Plug-ins that extend the capabilities of your Web pages are a mixed blessing. You risk losing your audience if you require them to jump through hoops to view your content.

APPLICATIONS FOR MULTIMEDIA

Web designers must always be considerate of the consumer. A happy customer will come back, but one who has been made to wait and is then offered goods that are irrelevant is likely to shop elsewhere. Because multimedia comes with a high price tag, it should be used sparingly and judiciously.

All too often Web authors include visual or moving elements on the page for the purpose of holding the user's attention. This approach is based on the assumption that Web users have short attention spans, which in many cases may be true. However, the solution is not to add gratuitous "eye candy" to your Web presentation, which may, in fact, command too much of the user's attention and detract attention from the main content of your page. When thinking about adding media to your Web pages, consider first and foremost the nature of your materials. Use images, animations, video, or sound only when relevant to your message.

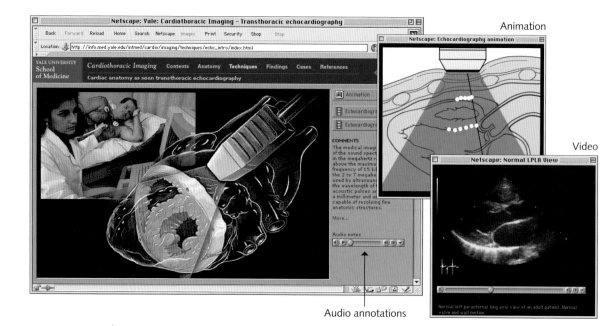

Animation

Video

Audio annotations

Bear in mind, too, that there are technical limitations to the delivery of audiovisual content via the Web. For example, long-duration video and video requiring smooth motion or clear details require large amounts of bandwidth to deliver and may tax the playback capacity of the user's machine. A significant amount of downsampling and compression is required to create a file that is small enough to be delivered via the Web. In some cases, these compromises may be too significant to warrant the effort. When you are considering adding multimedia to your pages, make sure the technology can meet the demands of your content. You don't want users to spend extra time and energy retrieving files that cannot be illustrative owing to limitations of the technology.

Also be wary of fledgling technologies. Plug-ins that allow users to see new and exciting things using their favorite browser software are constantly being introduced. This is especially true of multimedia; the options for encoding and delivering audio, animations, and video are dizzying. Although designers may be tempted to create files that employ the functionality offered by custom plug-ins, they should bear two things in mind. First, the bother and potential confusion of downloading and installing plug-ins will deter many users. Second, it is not prudent to create content in a custom file format that could quickly become obsolete. It is best to create your multimedia content in the standard formats for operating systems and browser software.

```
╔══════════ Unhandled File Type ══════════╗
║                                         ║
║   ⚠   Internet Explorer doesn't know how to handle the
║  /!\  type of file you have selected.
║                                         ║
║       You can choose to save this file to your disk or you
║       can configure a Helper Application for this file.
║                                         ║
║       MIME Type: application/x-shockwave-flash
║       File Name: uboat9c40.swf
║                                         ║
║   [ Cancel ]  [ Save File As... ]  [ Plugin ]  [ Application ]
║                                         ║
╚═════════════════════════════════════════╝
```

This somewhat conservative discussion of multimedia considerations needs one important qualification. If you are creating a site for a specific audience and not for global interests you will probably have more flexibility and can ask more from your users. You can require them to use specific browser software and plug-ins, and you can include data-intensive multimedia elements in your presentation. Say, for example, that your site is academic and your audience is a group of students or faculty with specialized interests. You are charged with the task of creating a custom site that fully addresses these interests, so function should define form. A foreign-language teaching site, for example, could contain bandwidth-intensive audio and video elements because the students who visit the site will use these multimedia elements to improve their abilities with the language. These students are not casual visitors; they are invested in the content, so they will tolerate lengthy download times and more demanding site interaction. And because your audience is defined and finite, you can take steps to ensure that they know what to expect and are prepared when they visit your site.

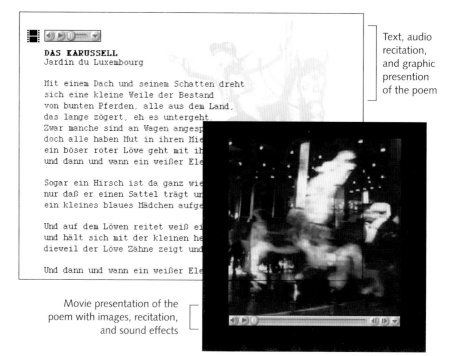

DAS KARUSSELL
Jardin du Luxembourg

Mit einem Dach und seinem Schatten dreht
sich eine kleine Weile der Bestand
von bunten Pferden, alle aus dem Land,
das lange zögert, eh es untergeht.
Zwar manche sind an Wagen angesp
doch alle haben Mut in ihren Mie
ein böser roter Löwe geht mit ih
und dann und wann ein weißer Ele

Sogar ein Hirsch ist da ganz wie
nur daß er einen Sattel trägt un
ein kleines blaues Mädchen aufge

Und auf dem Löwen reitet weiß ei
und hält sich mit der kleinen he
dieweil der Löwe Zähne zeigt und

Und dann und wann ein weißer Ele

Text, audio
recitation,
and graphic
presention
of the poem

Movie presentation of the
poem with images, recitation,
and sound effects

WEB MULTIMEDIA STRATEGIES

Simply because we *can* digitize hours' worth of analog video and stream it
out over the Web doesn't mean that we *should*. The value of having the text
of *Paradise Lost* on computer is not in making it available for reading—most
people prefer to read the work in print. We digitize texts in order to use the
strengths of computing, such as searching and linking, to enhance our understanding of the material. This holds true for multimedia, too: we need to
consider how best to use the computer and not simply translate analog video
and audio content to the computer screen. Networked multimedia requires
scaling and compression, which means that much of the content created for
analog delivery does not work well on the Web. The key to successful Web
multimedia is to tailor your content for Web delivery.

AUDIO ONLY

Audio is an extremely efficient way to deliver information. Consider a training video on measuring and weighing chemical compounds. Which track—
audio or video—would be the most important in conveying information? In
the sound track a narrator explains the procedure, and in the video track
someone is measuring and weighing compounds. Which track would you
remove if necessary? Which could stand alone? The audio track. Consider
enhancing your presentation with an audio component. Audio can be cap-
tured and optimized fairly easily, and it compresses well.

When recording original audio, take the time to do it right. Low-frequency background noises, such as the hum of a ventilation system, will be inseparable from your audio track; no amount of tweaking will eliminate it altogether. Remember, too, that the downsampling and compression you will have to perform to make your audio Web deliverable will emphasize any flaws in your recording.

SLIDE SHOWS

Slide shows are another method for delivering multimedia on the Web. In a slide show, you synchronize audio with still images. Through this approach you provide information via audio and add visual emphasis with still images. As an example, to present the training video mentioned above as a slide show, you would use video editing software to synchronize the narration with still images of the weighing and measuring procedure. Still images compress much more efficiently than video, and because slide shows do not require smooth motion, the movie frame rate can be low. This in turn means that you can devote more data to image quality and size.

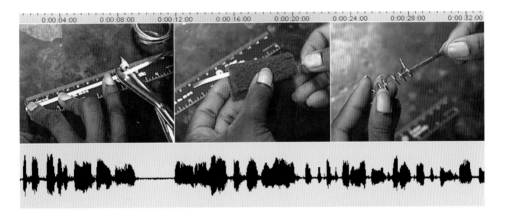

VIDEO

Video is the most challenging multimedia content to deliver via the Web. One second of uncompressed NTSC (National Television Standards Committee) video, the international standard for television and video, requires approximately 27 megabytes of disk storage space. The amount of scaling and compression required to turn this quantity of data into something that can be used on a network is significant, sometimes so much so as to render the material useless. If at all possible, tailor your video content for the Web.

- Shoot original video; that way you can take steps to create video that will compress efficiently and still look good at low resolution and frame rates.
- Shoot close-ups. Wide shots have too much detail to make sense at low resolution.

Wide shot, too much detail

Close shots work better at low resolution

- Shoot against a simple monochromatic background whenever possible. This will make small video images easier to understand and will increase the efficiency of compression.
- Use a tripod to minimize camera movement. A camera locked in one position will minimize the differences between frames and greatly improve video compression.
- Avoid zooming and panning. These can make low frame-rate movies confusing to view and interpret and can cause them to compress poorly.
- When editing your video, use hard cuts between shots. Don't use the transitional effects offered by video editing software, such as dissolves or elaborate wipes, because they will not compress efficiently and will not play smoothly on the Web.
- If you are digitizing material that was originally recorded for video or film, choose your material carefully. Look for clips that contain minimal motion and lack essential but small details. Motion and detail are the most obvious shortcomings of low-resolution video.

ANIMATION

Most Web animation requires special plug-ins for viewing. The exception is the animated GIF format, which is by far the most prevalent animation format on the Web, followed closely by Macromedia's Flash format. The animation option of the GIF format combines individual GIF images into a single file to create animation. You can set the animation to loop on the page or to play once, and you can designate the duration for each frame in the animation.

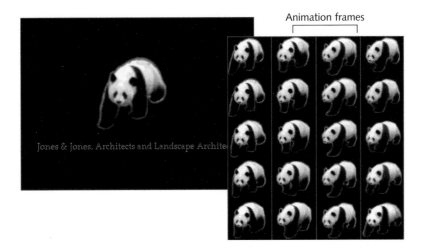

Animation frames

Animated GIFs have several drawbacks. One concerns the user interface. GIF animations do not provide interface controls, so users have no easy way to stop a looping animation short of closing the browser window. They also lack the means to replay nonlooping animation. Second, the animated GIF format does not perform interframe compression, which means that if you create a ten-frame animation and each frame is a 20 KB GIF, you'll be putting a 200 KB file on your page. And the final drawback is a concern that pertains to animations in general. Most animation is nothing more than a distraction. If you place animation alongside primary content you will simply disrupt your readers' concentration and keep them from the objective of your site. If you require users to sit through your spiffy Flash intro every time they visit your site, you are effectively turning them away at the door.

There is a place for animation on the Web, however. Simple animation on a Web site's main home page can provide just the right amount of visual interest to invite users to explore your materials. There, the essential content is typically a menu of links, so the threat of distraction is less than it would be on an internal content page. Also, subtle animation such as a rollover can help guide the user to interface elements that they might otherwise overlook. Animation can also be useful in illustrating concepts or procedures, such as change over time. When you have animation that relates to the content of your site, one way to minimize the potential distraction is to present the animation in a secondary window. This technique offers a measure of viewer control: readers can open the window to view the animation and then close the window when they're through.

PREPARING MULTIMEDIA

Multimedia places high demands on the network, the computer, and the user. The challenge thus lies in preparing files that are small enough to be accessible to the broadest possible audience yet are of sufficient quality to be worth the effort. To balance quality against accessibility you'll need to understand both the characteristics of different media formats and the limitations of delivering media in a networked environment, and you must be ready to compromise.

PROCESSING

Analog source generally comes with certain established characteristics. For example, CD-quality audio is sampled at 44.1 KHz, 16-bit stereo sound, and video is usually 640 × 480 pixels in dimension and plays at 30 frames per second (fps). However, analog source digitized at full resolution would require enormous amounts of disk storage and is far too large to be used on a network. One way to prepare media for network delivery is to reduce the data by, for example, downsampling the audio material to 11.025 KHz, 8-bit mono sound. This reduces file size but also substantially reduces quality. Another way to reduce file size is to apply compression.

Compression first eliminates redundant data from a file and then removes less important data to shrink file size still further. This process is achieved using algorithms, or "codecs" (short for compressors-decompressors), that handle the media compression and the decompression when it is played. The codecs that are used for Web delivery use lossy compression: the process removes data from the original source material. You should never compress material multiple times, because each process will lower the video quality.

In preparing media for Web delivery, you should aim for files that can be managed by the average network connection and desktop machine of your target audience. The key measure is the data rate, normally measured in kilobytes per second (KBps), which is the amount of data that is used to represent one second of movie playback. For users to play your files in real time without hiccups or delays, you need to set a data transmission rate that is slightly lower than the throughput of your users' connections.

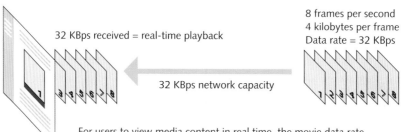

32 KBps received = real-time playback

8 frames per second
4 kilobytes per frame
Data rate = 32 KBps

32 KBps network capacity

For users to view media content in real time, the movie data rate must be less than or equal to the throughput capacity of their connection

Audio Processing

- Normalize. Audio files may lose amplitude and clarity in the digitizing process. To compensate you can use software to normalize your audio. This process finds the highest peak in a file and then amplifies the entire file to make that peak's volume 100 percent. This ensures that you are working with the loudest possible audio signal.
- Boost the midrange. Another way to enhance your Web audio is to use software with an equalizer function to boost the midrange frequencies slightly.
- Frequency. Reducing the frequency reduces the data required to represent the material, for example, from 44.1 KHZ to 22.050 KHZ.
- Depth. Sixteen-bit samples provide greater dynamic range but take up more space. Reducing the depth to 8-bit will reduce the file size.
- Channel. Be sure not to use stereo settings for a mono source. If your source does have stereo audio, you might consider switching to mono to reduce the data rate.
- Codec. Applying compression to an audio track may allow you to keep higher-quality audio frequency and depth settings.

Video

- Process the audio. Perform the audio normalizing and equalizing mentioned above.
- Trim clips. Make sure that your movie begins and ends with frames that make sense as still images. The first frame will appear on the user's screen while the movie is loading, and the last frame will remain on screen when the movie has finished. Take care that these images do not seem awkward out of the context of the movie.
- Crop. Use video editing software to crop out unwanted noise or borders from the movie image.

Digitized NTSC video   Crop to remove unwanted borders and video noise

- Scale. Most Web video is sized to quarter-screen (320 × 240 pixels) or smaller.
- Image quality. Reducing the image-quality setting of a movie reduces the data that is stored for each frame.
- Frame rate. Standard NTSC video has a frame rate of 30 fps. Most Web video is set to about 10 fps.
- Codec. Some codecs compress more efficiently than others do, though usually at the expense of image quality.
- Custom filters. Compression software provides filters that reduce the differences between frames, permitting more efficient compression.
- Audio. The audio track of video can be downsampled and/or compressed to reduce the overall movie data rate.

DELIVERY

The technology of networked media consists of three main components: the server, the network, and the client machine. These three components must work in tandem to deliver good Web multimedia to the desktop. It makes no difference how high-end your video server and network are if your users are running low-end desktop machines that cannot handle the demands of playback.

The wildest of all these wild cards is bandwidth. If you purchase a high-end media server, you can expect a certain level of performance. You can predict playback performance on desktop machines. These elements are somewhat measurable. But unless you are working with a dedicated network, bandwidth will be hugely variable and difficult to predict. Issues regarding bandwidth run from the basic configuration of your connection to the network to the amount of network traffic at any given time.

Given these variables, the parameters for creating and delivering Web multimedia are not easily defined. They will vary depending on the scope and content of your project. If you are creating a Web site for a corporate intranet, for example, your media can be more technologically demanding than if you send it worldwide over the Internet. The key is to be well acquainted with the configuration of your client base and prepare accordingly.

Streaming Streaming technology sends data to the desktop continuously but does not download the entire file. In the optimal scenario, the content is stored on a media server, which maintains a constant conversation with the client to determine how much data the user can support. Based on this information, the server adjusts the data stream accordingly and sends just enough data to the client.

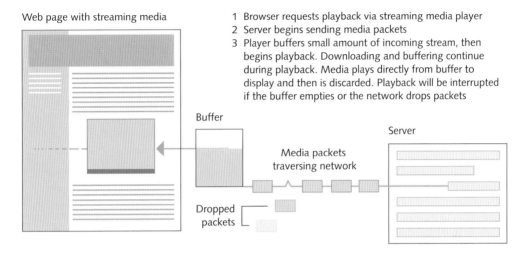

Web page with streaming media

1 Browser requests playback via streaming media player
2 Server begins sending media packets
3 Player buffers small amount of incoming stream, then begins playback. Downloading and buffering continue during playback. Media plays directly from buffer to display and then is discarded. Playback will be interrupted if the buffer empties or the network drops packets

Buffer

Server

Media packets traversing network

Dropped packets

Streaming offers many benefits, the first of which is random access. Streaming technology permits movies to be viewed at any point in the video stream. If your reader is accessing an hour's worth of video and wishes to view only the last five minutes, he or she can use the controls to move forward to the desired starting point. Another benefit is a lower storage demand on the client machine. Streaming media plays directly to the display; it is not stored in memory or on the hard drive.

The strengths of streaming are also its shortcomings. To play a movie in real time the player software needs to keep up with the incoming data sent from the server. As a result, if there are glitches in the network or if the client machine cannot handle playback, the data may simply be lost. Streaming playback requires significant processing power, so playback may be suboptimal if the processor has to drop frames to keep up with the incoming stream. Also, streaming media needs to be heavily compressed to create a file small enough to play in real time.

Downloading   Downloadable media is temporarily stored on the client machine in memory or on the hard drive. Most downloadable media is progressive, which means that the information necessary for playback is stored at the beginning of the file. Progressive download allows playback before the entire file has downloaded. Downloadable media is sent to the client using the same HTTP protocol as a Web page, so no special server is required. As long as the download speed stays above the data rate of the movie, playback will be uninterrupted.

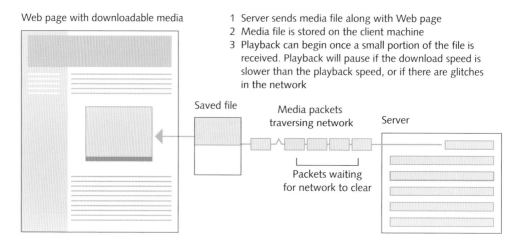

Web page with downloadable media

1 Server sends media file along with Web page
2 Media file is stored on the client machine
3 Playback can begin once a small portion of the file is received. Playback will pause if the download speed is slower than the playback speed, or if there are glitches in the network

Saved file

Media packets traversing network

Server

Packets waiting for network to clear

The quality of downloadable media is generally higher than that of streaming media. Because the data rate is not required to remain low enough to play the material in real time, more data can be devoted to image quality and motion. Downloadable media also has integrity: all the data in the original movie is contained in the downloaded version. This means that playback is predictable and that you can download the data onto your disk for future use.

The main drawback of downloadable media is the storage demand it places on the client machine. Even videos of short duration require many megabytes of storage. The other problem is that downloadable media does not allow random access. If you want to view only the last few minutes of a long clip you must wait for the entire clip to download. One solution to both of these problems is to split longer media segments into smaller chunks. This reduces the demands on the client machine and allows users more direct access to the material they want.

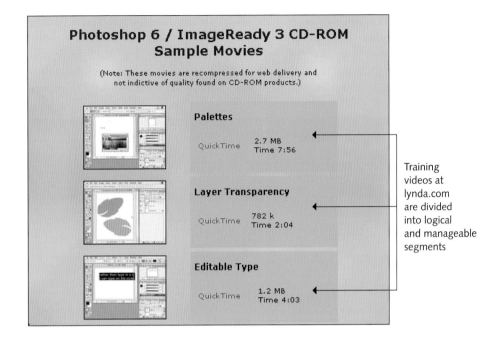

Photoshop 6 / ImageReady 3 CD-ROM Sample Movies

(Note: These movies are recompressed for web delivery and not indictive of quality found on CD-ROM products.)

Palettes

QuickTime   2.7 MB   Time 7:56

Layer Transparency

QuickTime   782 k   Time 2:04

Editable Type

QuickTime   1.2 MB   Time 4:03

Training videos at lynda.com are divided into logical and manageable segments

DESIGN AND MULTIMEDIA

The combination of low-bandwidth considerations and primitive interface options creates interesting design challenges for Web developers who wish to incorporate multimedia elements into their sites. Designers need to inform users when they are entering a high-bandwidth area and give them the tools they need to control their experience once in the area.

INFORM YOUR USERS

One aspect of the Web is that you don't always know where you're going or what you'll find there. For some this uncertainty is exciting. For many, it is annoying, particularly when a long wait is involved. Most frustrating, perhaps, is when you finally receive the requested page only to find that is not what you expected or that it contains materials in a format you are not set up to view. With content that is as technologically demanding as multimedia, it is especially important to give users enough information to make an informed decision *before they click,* so that they know what to expect and are prepared to receive your materials.

High-demand content such as large multimedia files should not be part of your basic page design. These materials should appear on secondary pages that are described and can be accessed from the main pages of your site. Make the menu page a plain HTML page that loads quickly and does not require special software. Include descriptive information about the materials along with previews such as still shots from the video. Include the run time for time-based media, and include the file size for materials that download.

In addition, fully explain any special software requirements for accessing the materials and provide a download link. Your users should have a clear idea of what your materials are before they begin to download. With a menu interface, users can confirm that their systems are properly configured and that they have enough bandwidth, time, and patience to load the materials.

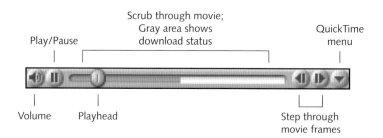

PROVIDE CONTROLS

Be sure to give users status information and controls when you are presenting multimedia materials. The QuickTime controller bar is an extremely effective interface element that provides both controls and status information. It allows users both to adjust the volume control and to play, stop, and scrub through a movie, and it provides information about the movie's download status.

If you don't include controls, users will hit your page with no way to control their viewing environment. For example, if a visitor is looking at your page at a public workstation and you have looping bird calls as a background sound without any control options, the visitor will experience an unsettling (and potentially embarrassing) moment when he or she cannot control interaction with your site. Many users in this situation will simply close the browser window to make the sound stop, which means that they never get to see the page content.

When designing a media interface, let interaction with your media be entirely user-driven. Always include user controls, such as a media controller bar, and make sure that users have a way to turn it off. Avoid prescribed playback options like auto play or looping that take control from the user. With auto play, for example, media files begin playing when a Web page is loaded. If the page has other elements, such as descriptive text, the user who wants just the text will find the video distracting. Design your media interface so that files play only when the user explicitly elects to initiate playback.

ACCESSIBILITY

It is nearly impossible to construct a multimedia presentation that will be accessible by every user on the World Wide Web. Whenever you put multimedia content on your Web pages you potentially shut out users. For example, vision-impaired users cannot see content such as graphics, video, or animations. To access visual content, they need a text alternative that can be spoken by a screen reader. Hearing-impaired users rely on content they can see, and so they need a visual alternative to any audible materials. Initiatives such as Section 508 and the Web Accessibility Initiative (WAI) have produced guidelines and mandates requiring that nontext content be rendered in an alternate format that is accessible to disabled users, such as text captions for audible content and text descriptions of visual content. This is why it is particularly important when planning for multimedia content to consider users with disabilities: both technology-disabled users who are connecting to the Internet via slow modems on outdated machines and physically disabled users for whom multimedia content may be out of reach.

Alternate versions   The best way to ensure that your materials are accessible is to provide alternate versions designed to accommodate different users. For example, when creating Web video using QuickTime, developers can link different versions of their movie saved at varying levels of quality and compression. Then, when a user requests the movie via a Web page, QuickTime sends the version that the user's network connection can best accommodate. This approach supports divisions in technology resources, but alternate views also benefit those who are excluded from multimedia for physical reasons. By providing alternate views of your multimedia content, your information becomes accessible to people who cannot appreciate it in its native format because of physical limitations.

Text is the most widely accessible content there is. For physically disabled users, text can be magnified or read by special software or rendered by a braille reader. For those with technology limitations, text loads quickly and can be viewed on nongraphical browsers. Another strength of text over media content is that it can be read and indexed by search engines and translated into other languages. The best alternate, then, to multimedia content is the written word. For instance, if you are providing video content on your site, the simplest alternate to include is a text transcript of the audio track for hearing-impaired users. An even better approach would be to use the text as captions synchronized with the video. To address the needs of visually impaired users, you could also include a text description of the video track, either as a separate audio track or as text. Or simplify the materials by reducing the video track to a series of still images synchronized with the audio for users with reduced vision or cognitive difficulties.

Video with captions

Audio transcript

At minimum, you can use basic HTML to give disabled users information about multimedia content. For example, you can use the ALT parameter to include a short description of the animation in your applet or animated GIF HTML code. Because almost all browsing devices can handle text, if you include this basic descriptive text, users who have their Web pages read to them will at least be able to understand the function of the visual content.

REFERENCES

Brewer, Judy, ed. 2001. *How people with disabilities use the Web.* http://www.w3c.org/WAI/EO/Drafts/PWD-Use-Web (31 March 2001).

Chisholm, Wendy, Gregg Vanderheiden, and Ian Jacobs, eds. 1999. *Web content accessibility guidelines 1.0.* http://www.w3c.org/TR/WAI-WEBCONTENT/wai-pageauth.html (17 January 2001).

CPB/WGBH National Center for Accessible Media. *Rich media resource center.* http://ncam.wgbh.org/richmedia (29 March 2001).

Kelsey, Logan, and Jim Feeley. 2000. Shooting video for the Web. *DV* (February). http://www.dv.com/magazine/2000/0200/videoforweb0200.html (28 March 2001).

Nielsen, Jakob. 1995. *The alertbox: Current issues in Web usability.* http://www.useit.com/alertbox.

———.1999. *Designing web usability: The practice of simplicity.* Indianapolis, Ind.: New Riders.

Simpson, Ron. 1998. *Cutting edge Web audio.* Upper Saddle River, N.J.: Prentice Hall.

Stern, Judith, and Robert Lettieri. 1999. *QuickTime Pro for Macintosh and Windows.* Berkeley, Calif.: Peachpit.

Terran Interactive. 1995–2000. *Cleaner 5 User Manual.* San Jose, Calif.: Terran Interactive. [See also http://www.terran-int.com]

———. 1999. How to produce high-quality QuickTime. San Jose, Calif.: Terran Interactive. [See also http://www.terran-int.com/QuickTime/Article]

Waggoner, Ben. 1999. Making great Web video. *DV* (October). http://www.dv.com/magazine/1999/1099/webvideo1099.pdf (28 March 2001).

Index

Illustration Credits

Physics at Yale University home page. www.yale.edu/physics. Copyright © 2001 Yale University. All rights reserved.

Argus Center for Information Architecture home page. argus-acia.com. Copyright © 2000 Argus Center for Information Architecture.

Salon.com Tech & Business page. www.salon.com. Copyright © 2001 Salon.com. Reprinted with permission of Salon Media Group.

Iowa State University home page. www.iastate.edu. Copyright © 2001 Iowa State University.

Yale Engineering home page. www.eng.yale.edu. Copyright © 2001 Yale University. All rights reserved.

THOMAS home page. The Library of Congress THOMAS Web site is in the public domain.

Guggenheim Museum home page. www.guggenheim.org. Guggenheim Museum website © 2000 The Solomon R. Guggenheim Foundation, New York.

W3C World Wide Web Consortium home page. www.w3.org. Copyright © 1994–2001 World Wide Web Consortium (Massachusetts Institute of Technology Laboratory for Computer Science, Institut National de Recherche en Informatique et en Automatique, Keio University). All rights reserved. http://www.w3.org/Consortium/Legal/.

The Atlantic Online home page. www.theatlantic.com. Copyright © 2001 by The Atlantic Monthly Group.

Yale–New Haven Hospital page footer. www.ynhh.org. Copyright © 2001 Yale–New Haven Hospital. All rights reserved.

WD+D proposal for Yale–New Haven Hospital intranet interface. Copyright © 2001 Yale University. All rights reserved.

Yale School of Medicine, WD+D, and ITSMed pages. info.med.yale.edu, its.med. yale.edu/wdd, and its.med.yale.edu. Copyright © 2001 Yale University. All rights reserved.

Yale–New Haven Hospital home and Cardiac Services pages. www.ynhh.org. Copyright © 2001 Yale–New Haven Hospital. All rights reserved.

Yale–New Haven Hospital home, Medical Professionals, and Children's Hospital pages. www.ynhh.org. Copyright © 2001 Yale–New Haven Hospital. All rights reserved.

IKEA site index. www.IKEA-usa.com. Copyright © 2000–2001 Inter IKEA Systems B.V.

Bitstream site map. www.bitstream.com. Copyright © 2001 Courtesy of Bitstream, Inc., 215 First Street, Cambridge, MA 02142.

The Chronicle of Higher Education search page. www.chronicle.com. Copyright © 2001 The Chronicle of Higher Education. Reprinted with permission. This material may not be posted, published, or distributed without permission from The Chronicle.

Monterey Bay Aquarium map and directions page. www.montereybayaquarium.org. Copyright © 1999–2001 Monterey Bay Aquarium Foundation.

Palm.com error page. www.palm.com. Copyright © 2001 Palm, Inc. Palm is a trademark of Palm, Inc.

IBM home page. www.ibm.com. Copyright © 1994–2001 IBM Corporation. All rights reserved.

NOAA home page and internal pages. www.noaa.gov. National Oceanic and Atmospheric Administration.

IBM Education and Small Business Center pages. www.ibm.com. © 1994–2001 IBM Corporation. All rights reserved.

Academic Computing home page. www.dartmouth.edu/~ac. Copyright ©
2000–2001 Trustees of Dartmouth College.

Palm.com home page. www.palm.com. Copyright © 2001 Palm, Inc. Palm is a
trademark of Palm, Inc.

eBay home page. www.ebay.com. Copyright © 1995–2001 eBay, Inc. All rights
reserved.

CHAPTER 8: MULTIMEDIA

Introduction to Cardiothoracic Imaging Techniques pages. info.med.yale.edu/
intmed/cardio/imaging. Copyright © 2001 Yale University. All rights reserved.

Rainer Maria Rilke Das Karussell pages. www.dartmouth.edu/~germ3/rilke/. Copyright © 1997–2001 Trustees of Dartmouth College.

Cold Harvest: The Natural Ice Business in Rural Vermont still frames. Copyright ©
1995 R. Michael Murray.

Jones and Jones home page. www.jonesandjones.com. Copyright © 1997 Jones &
Jones Architects and Landscape Architects. Designed by John Van Dyke.

Cold Harvest: The Natural Ice Business in Rural Vermont still frames. Copyright ©
1995 R. Michael Murray.

Lynda.com Sample Movies page. www.lynda.com. Copyright © 2001 Lynda.com.

HubbleSite Beyond Hubble page. hubble.stsci.edu. Produced by the Space Tele-
scope Science Institute's Office of Public Outreach for NASA Contract
NAS5–26555.

NOVA Cancer Warrior pages. www.pbs.org/wgbh/nova. Copyright © 2001 WGBH
Educational Foundation. Reprinted Courtesy of NOVA/WGBH Boston.